T0295686

Praise for *Future Cultures*

'Brings clarity and depth to the urgent topic of building futures capabilities across society.' LUCY KIMBELL, PROFESSOR OF CONTEMPORARY DESIGN PRACTICES, CENTRAL SAINT MARTINS, UNIVERSITY OF THE ARTS LONDON

'The only book I've read which digs deep and offers practical, actionable tactics for success.' NICK FOSTER RDI, FORMER HEAD OF DESIGN, GOOGLE X

'Written by two of the best guides in the field and packed with practical wisdom and insights from industry experts, this will be my indispensable handbook for the path ahead.' JD D'CRUZ, CEO AT RSPO, AND FORMER HEAD OF STRATEGY AND INNOVATION, UN DEVELOPMENT PROGRAMME

'The authors offer important insights from their years of experience developing corporate cultures that neither seek nor ignore uncertainty. They are the perfect guides to embedding long-term thinking in organizational strategy.' JESSICA BLAND, DEPUTY DIRECTOR, CENTRE FOR THE STUDY OF EXISTENTIAL RISK, UNIVERSITY OF CAMBRIDGE

'Smith and Cox-Smith are expert futurists and humanists who set out practical principles and methods in this book to help teams and communities build a holistic culture of foresight to shape shared prosperous futures.' LINA SRIVASTAVA, FOUNDER, CENTER FOR TRANSFORMATIONAL CHANGE

'An excellent guide to thinking about how to successfully run a creative business – to solve problems in ways that jolt people and impact them in their day-to-day lives in surprising ways.' DEAN WEI, CHIEF CREATIVE OFFICER, CRISPIN PORTER & BOGUSKY LONDON

Future Cultures

How to build a future-ready organization through leadership

Scott Smith
Susan Cox-Smith

Publisher's note
Every possible effort has been made to ensure that the information contained in this book is accurate at the time of going to press, and the publishers and authors cannot accept responsibility for any errors or omissions, however caused. No responsibility for loss or damage occasioned to any person acting, or refraining from action, as a result of the material in this publication can be accepted by the editor, the publisher or the authors.

First published in Great Britain and the United States in 2023 by Kogan Page Limited

2nd Floor, 45 Gee Street
London
EC1V 3RS
United Kingdom

8 W 38th Street, Suite 902
New York, NY 10018
USA

4737/23 Ansari Road
Daryaganj
New Delhi 110002
India

www.koganpage.com

Kogan Page books are printed on paper from sustainable forests.

ISBNs
Hardback   978 1 3986 1237 2
Paperback   978 1 3986 1238 9
Ebook   978 1 3986 1236 5

British Library Cataloguing-in-Publication Data
A CIP record for this book is available from the British Library.

Library of Congress Cataloging-in-Publication Data
Names: Smith, Scott, 1967- author. | Cox-Smith, Susan, author.
Title: Future cultures : how to build a future-ready organization through leadership / Scott Smith, Susan Cox-Smith.
Description: London ; New York, NY : Kogan Page, 2023. | Includes bibliographical references and index.
Identifiers: LCCN 2023030402 (print) | LCCN 2023030403 (ebook) | ISBN 9781398612389 (paperback) | ISBN 9781398612372 (hardback) | ISBN 9781398612365 (ebook)
Subjects: LCSH: Corporate culture. | Organizational change. | Leadership.
Classification: LCC HD58.7 .S634 2023 (print) | LCC HD58.7 (ebook) | DDC 302.3/5—dc23/eng/20230629
LC record available at https://lccn.loc.gov/2023030402
LC ebook record available at https://lccn.loc.gov/2023030403

Typeset by Integra Software Services, Pondicherry
Print production managed by Jellyfish
Printed and bound by CPI Group (UK) Ltd, Croydon, CR0 4YY

To the other one.

Contents

About the authors

Scott Smith

Scott is founder and managing partner of Changeist, a futures consulting group based in Barcelona, Spain, operating globally. With nearly 30 years of professional experience as an analyst, writer, consultant, advisor and futurist, Scott leads the company's strategy, research and partnerships. In this role, he has worked with some of the world's largest brands, most progressive cultural institutions, governments and top NGOs. Scott previously led research and consulting teams for several boutique firms in Washington, DC, New York and London. He has worked in over 20 countries, in multiple languages, and led development of several futures and innovation programmes at educational institutions in the US, Spain and the UAE. He has written for *The Atlantic*, *Quartz* and *WIRED UK*, had work exhibited in several museums, and spoken at dozens of conferences globally, including SXSW, Lift, Sónar+D and Sibos. Scott was the author of *How to Future: Leading and sense-making in an age of hyper-change*, for Kogan Page. He currently lives in Barcelona.

Susan Cox-Smith

Susan is partner and director, experience at Changeist, leveraging over 25 years of experience as a writer, designer, creative director, interactive producer and researcher. Susan seeks to enrich public engagement with possible futures. She oversees the design of and co-leads Changeist's capacity-building workshops, and the development of learning experiences, developing futuring skills in leaders from organizations including Microsoft, Netflix, JPMorganChase and NASA JPL. She also provides research, story consulting, narrative development, storyboarding and scriptwriting for exhibitions and future immersive concepts for international clients. She has written for *The Next Web* and *How We Get to Next*, and appeared on several podcasts to discuss futures and trends. Susan has presented at a number of academic conferences, moderated panel discussions, and presented her and Changeist's work in New York, Vienna and Singapore. She was the contributing editor on *How to Future: Leading and sense-making in an age of hyperchange.* She lives in Barcelona.

Foreword

The theory of economics does not furnish a body of settled conclusions immediately applicable to policy. It is a method rather than a doctrine, an apparatus of the mind, a technique for thinking, which helps the possessor to draw correct conclusions. JOHN MAYNARD KEYNES (*THE GENERAL THEORY OF EMPLOYMENT, INTEREST AND MONEY*, 1922)

I was trained in a mix of economics, philosophy and political science. This quote from Keynes remains one of my favourites – not least because most of the 'settled conclusions' from my undergraduate years have either been forgotten or overtaken by the real world. Even some of the methods and apparatus of the mind that I learnt have proven incomplete at best – theories of incentives have been complemented by the behavioural revolution, and marginalist thinking by more emergent, nonlinear approaches.

One technique for thinking that has endured, however, is the basic distinction between demand and supply. Susan and Scott's previous book *How to Future* (together with the equally brilliant Madeline Ashby) is one of the best I have seen on the supply and production of futures – how to do it rigorously and well. This book addresses the equally important second half of the equation – how to cultivate good demand for futures; that is, literate, informed consumption by organizations in which futures work is done.

Susan and Scott rightly focus on culture as a core, grounding concept. Working in government and offering occasional advice to friends in businesses and non-profits regularly confirms for me the truth of Peter Drucker's adage that culture eats strategy for breakfast – what more might one expect of futures, strategy's sometimes vague and mildly eccentric cousin? When I can eke out time, I try to do pro bono work for organizations of which I am particularly fond. In one of them, a community of Camaldolese Benedictine hermit monks living off the Big Sur coast in California, our discussions on long-term futures are deeply visceral, since every few years they are affected by climate-change-induced road collapses and closures. They regularly quote Drucker back at me, telling me that one of the most insightful things they have taken from my futures workshops (yes, even monks need to plan!) has been on the importance of culture, without which they know any amount of planning will be futile.

It was encouraging to see Susan and Scott begin their discussion of culture with a chapter on people and mindsets. People, with all their vagaries and idiosyncrasies, are the cornerstones of cultures. If you take away just one thing from this book, make it the multi-layered acronym HAPI (no spoilers here), a state of being all organizations should aspire to for their staff. In the Singapore government, where I was the first Head of an internal think tank, the Centre for Strategic Futures, people are similarly the focus of our futures work: they are trained in regular courses called 'FutureCraft', and both scenario planning and design techniques are taught as basic policy literacies in the first cross-government training attended by those identified as leadership talent. Not everyone turns into a fan, but this is still a core culture-building tool: at best, we get a few foresight champions; at worst, sceptics learn the vocabulary and don't become immovable obstacles.

Much of the rest of the book also resonates with my experience. As a poet, I readily confess to a deep love for the chapter on language and communication – and could not agree more that the core function of futures is to shape and shift collective vocabulary. Singapore's effort with futures is now a decades-long project, but I still find myself smiling when phrases like 'driving forces', 'critical uncertainties', 'wild cards', 'black swans' and the names of various other inhabitants of the futures menagerie roll off my colleagues' tongues utterly and totally naturally.

The chapter on tools and knowledge, with its discussion of decentralizing tools like card games, crowdsourcing, Slack, Discord and DAOs, brought to mind one of my volunteering efforts, The Birthday Collective. The group comprises entirely volunteers who collect stories of Singapore, using them to galvanize thinking and action about the country's long-term prospects, and is deeply informed by futures and open space facilitation techniques. During the Covid-19 pandemic, when our volunteers could not meet in large groups, we undertook several experiments to 'think collectively' using Google Docs. After some minor teething challenges, this turned into an incredibly generative exercise, but it clearly only worked because we were building on strong friendships and common frames of reference. We had a culture of our own, which our online tools could enable, enrich and enhance – but could never replace.

Susan and Scott reminded me of many other personal experiences in the great fight for better futures (and make no mistake, the fight is worthwhile). Their references to the importance of space and experience underscore how space is not just physical but mental and emotional: the result not just of dedicated rooms with whiteboards, markers and post-its, but also the freedom to probe existing ideas and introduce new ones, however odd they might seem. This can be done with guest speakers, by circulating articles, even using videos and visual recorders to prompt new thinking via non-verbal communications. Everything is an experience, really, even reading a document – which prompted one of my CSF teams to expand their mental space by presenting material for one project in fictitious, futuristic versions of articles from well-known publications.

When Susan and Scott refer to rules and norms reinforcing culture, I recall how various Singapore agencies established dedicated futures meetings to build and sustain exactly such norms: the Strategic Futures Network (SFN) of senior officers from the whole-of-government level, but also many subsidiary networks like the SFN Sandbox (for more junior officials). There are also futures-oriented meetings that eschew the term futures from their names, so that potential critics are kept at bay: one agency referred to a 'monthly policy review meeting' while another held monthly 'policy coordination, strategy and review' meetings: first to build, and later to sustain, an anticipatory and futures-oriented culture.

When the authors mention networks and ecosystems, I found myself thinking of how such groups are not just internal to an organization (e.g. comprising futurists and other allies), but can also (even often!) be found outside. In Singapore, government futurists learnt a while ago that some of our best allies are fellow citizens, not other government employees, leading to many public engagement projects to harness ideas about the future: Our Singapore Conversation (2012), Singapore Together (2020) and most recently, Forward Singapore (2023). These have not been described as futures projects, but have distinct futures elements in their ethos.

I share these examples to illustrate how broadly and deeply Susan and Scott's nuanced ideas jive with my lived reality as a futurist. Governments can be difficult beasts to move – Weber was not wrong to speak of the 'iron cage of bureaucracy'. But they can also house cultures and subcultures of passion, enthusiasm and absorptive capacity for good futures, many of which I have been privileged to work with. This book is a must-read for anyone interested in the methods, apparatus of the mind and techniques of thinking (and feeling, and doing!) to grow, sustain and eventually coalesce these cultures with their organizations' broader work.

Aaron Maniam
Fellow of Practice and Director
Digital Transformation Education Programme
Blavatnik School of Government, University of Oxford

Acknowledgements

This book is a direct product of our previous book, *How to Future*, written and released a mere three years ago (though it feels like yesterday). We write about this more inside, so won't spoil it here, but it's worth saying that this comes as a direct product of the experiences we've had as a team, teaching and discussing the concepts and approaches from that first book with workshops and in classrooms all over the world and on Zooms all over the Web, as well as from applying them ourselves since its publication. While that work came well over a decade into our practice, it had the effect of focusing our thinking, while also becoming an object that sparked conversations and consideration of how futures work takes place inside organizations, in ways that just applying our knowledge in practice probably wouldn't have.

Practitioners and experimentalists at heart, we tend to do first, and think to document later. But also being listeners and observers, we take note of the experiences we and our partners have, and the debates and questions that arise along the way. More than any specific outcome, we're driven to unpack and understand these multiple experiences of wrangling the future, how people and organizations understand them, and how to make them more productive. Teaching is just a means to this end, an opportunity to better understand how others see their futures, and how they find best uses for the tools we use to help uncover them.

Writing this book has afforded us another valued experience. Your authors have spent several decades working together in a professional context, and like any professional partnership, that often means one person front of stage more than the other, one person louder, more chatty or more visible than the other. We know numerous partnerships like this. That's how personalities go.

What often isn't seen is how we come together after the workshop, video call, presentation or meeting, to share, digest and, as we talk a great deal about here, collectively make sense of what's been seen, heard and done. That quiet, collaborative sensemaking has been the critical component of our practice, relying as it does on two distinct – but as it turns out, highly-complementary – points of view. It has also sustained a personal partnership of over 30 years, without which the professional one wouldn't be possible. This book is an overdue product and small marker of that partnership, and benefits immeasurably from it.

The professional side of this, and a good bit of the personal, has benefitted from the wider contribution of a wonderful network of peers, partners and colleagues. Considering the scope of this work, a broad range of people contributed directly and indirectly to our work. Some of these individuals helped us shoot the rapids of the pandemic (to borrow a phrase from futures history) as a small business, as individual professionals and humans, and also deserve our deepest thanks. We don't have to tell anyone who's lived through the past few years that this hasn't been easy.

We gladly go on record to say we wouldn't have any of this to offer without the hard work, tolerance, mentoring, presence, generosity, moral support, friendship, daring, curiosity, creativity, inspiration, examples, insights, challenges, endurance, indulgence, referrals, patronage and/or humour of many, many friends and colleagues.

We have continued to benefit greatly from a very supportive segment of the futures and futures-adjacent fields. Among these friends we can point to the following who have in some way shaped, enhanced or otherwise left their mark on our work. They are: Dr Noah Raford, Traci Croft, Madeline Ashby, Samantha Culp, Aarathi Krishnan, John Willshire and Helen Willshire of Smithery, Lily Higgins, Dr Kristin Alford, Alisha Bhagat, Ariel Muller, Lina Srivastava, Tobias Revell, Georgina Voss, Dr Richard Sandford, Dr Malka Older, the Near Future Laboratory team of

Julian Bleecker, Fabien Girardin and Nicolas Nova, Nick Foster, Dr Michelle Kazprzak, Johannes Kleske, Igor Schwarzmann, Fred Scharman, Greg Lindsay, Dr Anthony Townsend, Jay Owens, Anab Jain and John Ardern of Superflux, Simone Rebaudengo, Chor Pharn Lee, Honor Harger, nik gaffney and Maja Kuzmanovic of FoAM, Tina Auer and Tim Boykett of Time's Up, Dr Lucy Kimbell, Nicholas Davis, Dr Aaron Maniam, JD D'Cruz, Shumon Basar, Brendan McGetrick, Lukasz Alwast, James Andrews, Marko Russiver, Zhan Li, Dr Pedro Russo, Angeliki Kapoglou, Christian Ervin, Cassie Robinson, Rachel Coldicutt, Annette Mees, Sara Watson, Dan Hill, Immy Kaur, Dr Jake Dunagan, Dr Stuart Candy, Toshi Hoo, Brendan Caffin, Noriko Wynn, Ben Cerveny, Bridgette Engeler, Pratkeesha Singh, Dan Goods, David Delgado, Harper Reed, Gabriella Gomez-Mont, Christopher Schroeder, Catherine Feischi, Helen Walters, Jose Luis De Vicente, Kevin Slavin, Viktoria Modesta, Mitch Carter Jafery, Thomas Ermacora, Khaliya, Thomas Philbeck, Sougwen Chung, Lydia Nicholas and NFG at large.

In Dubai, we thank HE Khalfan Belhoul, Dr Patrick Noack, Mariam Al Muhairi, Tala Anshasi, Rowdha Al Sayegh, Sara Alsuwaidi, Asma Ahmed and team at Dubai Future Foundation, as well as Majid Alshamsi, Rawdha Moussa Sabah and team at The Executive Office for inviting us to work with so many wonderful people over the years.

Two teams in particular stress-tested our thinking about technical and social practice in the past few years; they are: Celia Hannon, Louis Stupple-Harris, Laurie Smith and Florence Engasser of Nesta, and Narue Shiki, Clarice Wilson, Darah Aljoudar, Vanessa Howe-Jones, the Futures Fellows, and the Sustainable Finance Hub team of UNDP.

We also give deep thanks to Mick Costigan, Henry Cooke, Libby Miller, Jeanette Kwek, Cheryl Chung, Olivier Desbiey, Alifeya Najibee, John Wise, Joanna Lepore, Dan Silveira, Roosevelt Faulkner, Meghan McGrath, Jim Maltby, John Carney, Dawn

McLeod and others for sharing their time, expertise and insights as we researched this book.

Thanks also to Matt James of Kogan Page who responded to a half-pitch enthusiastically on our first call, then waited patiently for months as we sharpened that to an actual proposal. And we continue to be grateful to the global Kogan Page team who bring these words to people who might find them interesting.

Lastly, we thank our families for understanding that we frequently disappear into our work, fall down research rabbit holes, walk and talk about world events instead of what's going on directly around us, read far too many newspapers, spend too much time on long-haul flights, live on too many time horizons that aren't the present, and have exotic jobs they can't explain to their friends. To the young ones, we're immensely proud of you.

Introduction

Timing the future

A funny thing happened on the way to the future. Well, not funny in the humour sense, but funny as in *differing from the anticipated*. In 2019, following almost two decades of very diverse work in what we could broadly summarize as the field of foresight, we (here, Scott Smith with Madeline Ashby and Susan Cox-Smith) decided to write a book detailing what we learnt from both implementing and teaching a range of approaches, and to impart practical, tactical advice on the practice as well as the processes of applied prospection. Most of this learning happened in the context of our work within Changeist, a futures research and consulting company Scott and Susan founded in 2007. We gathered our notes from extensive global project work, and slides from many years of teaching these topics, and pitched the book. After a few meetings, we found a happy home for what was eventually titled *How to Future: Leading and sense-making in an age of hyperchange*, with the publishers of this work.[1]

In brief, *How to Future* was written with a couple of objectives in mind. The first was to produce a simple, accessible guide to futuring, that is, the ongoing process of sensing, sense-making, exploring and assessing impacts of possible futures, typically in order to identify emerging risks or opportunities and discover preferred pathways forward, using an ongoing, iterative approach with a flexible process. This process, pictured in Figure 0.1, is one we consistently apply in all of our work, regardless of the breadth or depth of exploration. We begin by framing or setting parameters of exploration (how far out in time, where, for whom?). Then, we collect data and information that informs our understanding of the future, which is then mapped in different ways to develop new insights, and describe a few alternative future stories and insights for strategy, then finally assess, post-engagement, for how fit for purpose the process was.

How to Future laid out some fundamentals of what futuring is, and how the practice of prospection has shifted and continues to transform as a structured set of anticipatory and imaginative practices. It discusses where foresight and futuring sit in the strategy and innovation worlds, defines key building blocks, explains a non-exhaustive set of tools and methods, and provides examples of how to apply them in various ways. When we began writing, there seemed to be a distinct lack of such a guide in the world, and this impression has continued to be reinforced by the many comments we've received directly and via social media since its release.

The second objective of writing *How to Future* was to document our own real-world experience of applied futuring in a wide variety of contexts and scales around the world, over the course of a decade. This was based on an observation that this kind of tactical knowledge is very often left out of texts and workshops on foresight methods, the literature on what's often called 'futures literacy,'[2] and from other resources and instruction around futures and foresight. In short, various sources and programmes may tell you what to do, but finding out when to do it, when and how to choose between approaches, and how to

FIGURE 0.1   Updated *How to Future* process model

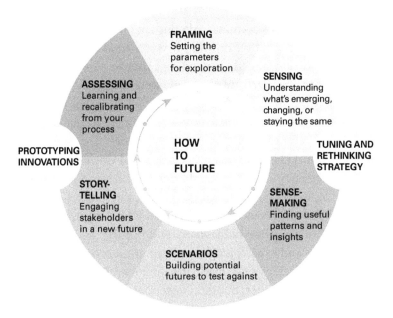

FRAMING
Setting the
parameters
for exploration

SENSING
Understanding
what's emerging,
changing, or
staying the same

ASSESSING
Learning and
recalibrating
from your
process

**HOW
TO
FUTURE**

**TUNING AND
RETHINKING
STRATEGY**

**PROTOTYPING
INNOVATIONS**

**STORY-
TELLING**
Engaging
stakeholders
in a new future

**SENSE-
MAKING**
Finding useful
patterns and
insights

SCENARIOS
Building potential
futures to test against

Source: Changeist (2020)

do it well in real-world situations full of people, politics and shifting contexts isn't easy, and it isn't taught in school.

Part of the pitch for *How to Future* was... timing. 2020 was shaping up to be a monumental year globally: major elections in the US and dozens of other countries, the implementation of Brexit, brewing conflicts, bigger leaps in artificial intelligence and other important technologies, a growing reckoning with climate change, and more. If you like your rationale served numerologically, round-numbered years are milestones in major corporate or government strategies, and tend to take on a life of their own. 2020 was going to be a big, transitional year, we promised, making it propitious timing for the release of a new book about wrangling the future.

'Great!' said the publisher, and off we went to start research-ing, writing, editing and submitting chapters as 2019 came to a close, anticipating that 2020 would serve up some interesting disruptions.

Did it ever. Always a known risk, but unknowable in its timing, 2020 began with what we now know was a pandemic brewing in China and possibly already beyond that country's borders. In the opening weeks of 2020, while many were distracted by sabre-rattling between the US and Iran, a mutating virus was travelling along the networks of global travel and trade, rolling towards nearly every corner of an unsuspecting planet. The very same month the World Health Organization declared Covid-19 a 'Public Health Emergency of International Concern', on the other shore of Lac Léman, in the same canton of Geneva, the World Economic Forum (WEF) rolled out its annual Global Risk Report, providing a snapshot of the perceived risks its 800-member community of global leaders and experts judged to be of greatest concern.[3]

Infectious diseases only made it to number 10 in the top 10 risks in terms of impact, but didn't even feature in the top 10 in terms of likelihood. Laudably, climate action failure was front and centre of that year's risk matrix, followed by concerns about infrastructure fragility and, relatedly, cyberattacks. Ironically, issues such as energy price shocks, unmanageable inflation, asset bubbles and financial failures were deemed to be more edge risks in the WEF model. To be fair, they probably seemed so in late 2019 as leaders' viewpoints were being compiled for the report.

In the three years since the Covid-19 pandemic began, the deaths of over 6.6 million people worldwide have been attributed to Covid.[4] Billions more have seen their lives disrupted or changed forever by the pandemic. Supply chains seized up, laying bare the fragility of our hyper-connected modern condition. In the view of many analysts, instability created an opportunistic moment for the brutal Russian invasion of Ukraine. Crisis piled upon crisis. Chances are that as you're reading this, you, like us, are still managing one or more slip-streams of these compounding crises.

What 2020 meant for our preceding book was delay. With UK supply chains and much of retail shut down for stretches of the year, and many in professional work on furlough, the delicate specialist production and supply chains that move a work from edited manuscript to layout to proofing, printing, stocking and selling ground to a halt, despite the best efforts of all involved. We don't have to explain the irony of a book about how to deal productively and proactively with various futures as they emerge being waylaid by an unprecedented series of interlocking system failures and cascading impacts.

Eventually, the Herculean efforts of many near and far, from our publisher to healthcare workers, policy specialists, economists and everyday rank and file workers, to the many, many silent carers behind the scenes, the wheels slowly started turning again. *How to Future* rolled off the presses, and, far more importantly, global and national economies lurched forward again, despite a landscape littered with existential challenges.

Confronting a hyperobject

Along with its many disparate impacts, the shock of the pandemic triggered something not seen perhaps since the OPEC embargoes of the early 1970s: it forced organizations large and small to reckon with their lack of foresight capacity, knowledge, tools and, eventually, their overall posture towards the future, risk and uncertainty. In the 1970s, this uncertainty fuelled the development of scenario planning, which served as the methodological tent pole for strategic foresight for the following four decades. The pandemic brought scenario planning back to the fore as a tool with name recognition in C-suites, but it also generated a surge of demand for any and all types of future tools, skills, knowledge and learning.

Despite much of it being initially undirected, the nested shocks of the pandemic and its aftermath(s) sounded a very loud alarm across organizations of every size, from top global brands, to mid-sized firms, to SMEs and start-ups. Even as they scrambled to orient themselves to the crises, commercial firms weren't the first out of the gate. Governments and non-governmental organizations, as the first-responders to the unfolding emergency, worked to collect what knowledge and tools they had to build some sort of functional forward view.

For example, only a few months into the pandemic in early 2020, Changeist collaborator Madeline Ashby independently received a request to develop scenarios for the World Health Organization (WHO), specific to a vast and diverse region with broad disparities in wealth, access to technology and resources, cultural norms and public health practices. To inform those scenarios, she spoke to public health professionals from across the region, all of whom had the same goal – to ameliorate the worst of the crisis – while serving wildly different populations.

In these discussions, the stakes of the crisis became immediately and painfully clear: this event was going to change the world. It had already changed the worlds of the people she interviewed and facilitated workshops for. Some of them had been evacuated from their workplaces; others were suddenly at home, estimating the probable numbers of orphans in their region while worrying about where their own children would go to school, how they would collaborate with colleagues previously met in an office or symposium, and many more considerations that came home to most of us in next few months.

Numerous other organizations reached out directly for scenarios, hoping to map ways out of a crisis that was still unfolding. Hundreds of scenario sets were generated in the opening 12 months of the pandemic, using dozens of variations on accepted methodologies. 'Five scenarios for the post-coronavirus sports industry', 'Impact, scenarios and perspectives for the international postal sector', 'Covid-19 recovery scenarios for fashion and luxury brands'. Name a sector and there are probably a myriad of scenario reports still gathering dust on a shelf somewhere.

And yet, many of these attempts at generating foresight strategies lacked foresight itself. They were almost all built without knowing certain key inputs and true critical uncertainties, or key questions that needed to be asked. Covid was a nail of uncertain dimensions. The issues of transmissibility, responsiveness to long-term treatment and projections for numbers of deaths were largely unknown. Scenarios became the hammer. Credit to those who asked useful questions, but the rush to assess possible damage and find an attainable exit exposed the lack of knowledge, skill, resources and tools for dealing with what philosopher Timothy Morton terms a 'hyperobject', a situation so complex, massive and entangled that it is hard to conceive of its true nature, much less solve.[5]

many attempts at generating foresight strategies lacked foresight itself.

Creating capacity for anticipation

Hiring in futures roles boomed in 2020, and has continued booming as 2023 opens. Of course, just having an internal manager of foresight or director of futures doesn't magically create capacity for critical prospection. The detailed inventory of needs and the acquisition of tools and skills even within a small team takes time and needs to be situated properly in the broader context of strategic decision making. Different approaches will be tried, and some are kept, some discarded. Most of all, inputs to these tools and processes are required: organizations need to gain access to intelligence about possible futures, so they can feed it into their long-term planning, or better yet, fully develop their own intelligence. Workflows and systems need to be thought out, knowledge accumulated and processes established. Good foresight needs a metaphorical engine, to go along with the slides and canvases.

Futuring is the ongoing process of sensing, sense-making, exploring and assessing impacts of possible futures, typically to identify emerging risks or opportunities, and find preferred pathways forward.

This is, in part, how *How to Future* came to be. The book and the capacity-building programme we created around it were developed to help teams or individuals get up to speed quickly on futuring skills, by outlining a selection of tools to use, as well as exploration of a range of futuring approaches and methods. We at Changeist soon found ourselves working with everyone from the largest and most leading-edge technology groups in the world, who were attempting to develop solutions to long-term planetary challenges, to small groups and even social entrepreneurs and charities working to feed, house and keep safe people in nearby streets and neighbourhoods.

Tools aren't everything

This concentrated exercise in getting capabilities into the hands of those who needed and desired them made one thing clear for us above all else: new tools and methods are valuable, and necessary in a crisis where the absence of them can actively harm or delay positive action, but they aren't the whole picture. These tools and practices, used by a handful of people in a given organization, won't stick without a serious shift in that organization's culture. An individual or small team may be trained to effectively imagine and design for possible futures, with new awareness and attitudes about opportunity, uncertainty and risk, yet, if the rest of an organization remains rooted in the present, this effectively quarantines the future. The lack of a deeper, wider future-facing culture creates a disconnect, relegating this capacity into the isolated islands where it initially

new tools and methods are valuable but they aren't the whole picture.

takes root. This isolation can stall, or even worse, terminate, any real progress towards becoming future-ready, negating the investment in building foundational capacity.

We are not in normal times, and the risks are not normal either. We are in a critical window where, as one designer interviewed for this book put it, 'the embodied experience of being surprised by the future' has made the uncertainty and complexity of dealing with futures very, very real, personally as well as professionally, for nearly everyone. Resources may be temporarily devoted to acting on this experience to change how organizations think and perform, but, the pressure of dealing with immediate challenges, juggling new ones and simply staying afloat may close this window quickly. Recency bias may overwhelm commitment to becoming more effective at aiming into the future before we attempt to know it.[6]

Where this book comes in

Whether it's setting attitudes towards risk, sensing disruptive change from the edges, or 'pre-hearsing' uncomfortable or unfamiliar possibilities, effective future-shaping can't take root without holistic change in the way organizations think about, talk about and approach the future. It can't happen if only one small team or lone individual has responsibility for it.

effective future-shaping can't take root without holistic change

We wrote this book to help teams and organizations overcome that hurdle, and to nurture deeper skills for awareness and anticipation, change the way leaders consider risk and uncertainty, foresee disruptive change before it arrives. *Future Cultures* is meant to explore in greater detail how organizations can fundamentally rewire their cultures to be more fluent, agile and comfortable when dealing with what comes next.

Our broader objective is to provide you, as a futures leader, with an adaptable framework for developing *cultural infrastructure for sense-making* within your team or organization – not re-engineering or restructuring, but for building a strong system for sensing and understanding the world as it's changing, in order to become more anticipatory and less reactive, and to *drive better decisions* from bottom to top in any organization.

Our own experience, plus experts

Driven by our own direct experiences inside and outside Changeist over the past 20 years, working in applied futures around the world, we invited practitioners and professionals from over a dozen companies, governments, agencies, foundations and NGOs across the Americas, Europe, Asia and the Middle East to provide us with insights of their own experience building a futures culture in their organizations. *Future Cultures* intends to highlight both the obstacles and opportunities that leaders, teams and organizations can face in the real world while working to scale up their futuring capabilities, practices and mindsets. Rather than issue opaque advice and one-size-fits-all recommendations, we've tried to go a bit deeper to look at both common and sector-specific fail points that create barriers to building a future culture, and explore the tactics and strategies used by those on the front line of futuring, as well as our own practical experience.

Throughout *Future Cultures*, we try to bring as much of the real world into the mix as possible to provide you, the reader, with some practical insights grounded in real cases, because concepts, while interesting on their own, truly get shaped, changed and strengthened in application to actual business, policy and design problems. The future doesn't happen within a vacuum of slides, speeches and symposia, but in sense-making, decision-taking, and the actions of people, teams, groups and leaders – in actual cultures.

Who this book is for

We wrote *How to Future* for a very wide spectrum of audiences: new or existing futures and innovation teams, individuals, groups, collaborators, students, creatives and more. *Future Cultures* is very much written for the same groups, although perhaps at a more advanced level of applications of the approaches outlined in *How to Future*. The dynamics, tactics, strategies and stories herein are intended to help push the edges of a futures community within an organization or world, or simply to expand the scope of application. It's designed to help readers learn from the insights and practices of those who have taken similar paths, through different or maybe even familiar challenges, and how they have succeeded in those efforts.

The aim of this book is not to convince anyone to care about the future and do something about it. That should be a given. We assume you are reading it because you've taken that step, or plan to, want to build a durable, flexible capability and catalyse that capability in others. *Future Cultures* was written to help anyone who is trying to guide their organization towards a preferable future – and possibly transform it into a present-day organization operating in a highly anticipatory and future-aware state. Our goal here is to help you build your capacity for seeding and growing stronger, more durable, accessible and successful anticipatory practices, customs, ideas and behaviours within a team or organization.

This book is not only for leaders in the hierarchical sense – though we strongly welcome top-down sponsorship and guidance of any futuring efforts – or support from those with resources and influence. In the context of futuring, we strongly believe leadership is situational, and can be shown by those who are newer and more inexperienced in futures and foresight work as well as by well-positioned veterans.

Leadership may be desirable in or executed by the head of a unit or team, but it also may reside with anyone who takes on the initiative to explore possible futures, or anyone who brings new insights and sense-making to such an exploration. When we say 'futures leader' we mean all of the above. This book is for anyone who wants to expand their futures practice, create and nurture a future culture and extend the community of those in your organization who care about the future, and want to live and act on that investment every day. That's leadership.

How this book is structured

This book was designed to follow the development of a future culture from its zero-point, the early pioneers of any new futures practice in an organization, team or community, and follow it along the key conduits of culture change within an organization into environments, practices, rituals and codes, into the supporting networks that connect and enrich that culture. We represent them as nested layers (Figure 0.2), but they are actually more like arteries that create a network through an organization. We build on this model later in Chapter 7. Throughout the book, we share our own collective experience, and provide both insights and examples from experts at the front line of future culture in high-performing organizations around the world.

Looking forward from this point:

Chapter 1 – From function to culture – we start by looking at how we got here in the first place. Isn't forecasting the future just a job for a few magicians in a corner cubicle? What happens when everyone has the responsibility for futuring – when 'to future' is a verb, an ongoing activity for the whole organization, rather than just an occasional report? This chapter looks at some of the structural barriers in the way of making the future a cultural norm, and drivers for creating a culture now.

Chapter 2 – People and mindset – people are at the core of any future culture. What qualities are needed in anticipatory teams, and what capabilities can be harnessed in wider networks? What should you look for in both core futuring teams and in cultivating allies?

Chapter 3 – Language and communication – how we talk about the future matters. Language creates the linkage between people and is the carrier for culture. Can we use language to make us more sensitive to and comfortable with what the future may be?

Chapter 4 – Tools and knowledge – how can wider networks of knowledge and insights be captured, and awareness of future possibilities and impacts be socialized? New tools can play an important role in harnessing collective knowledge about indicators of change.

Chapter 5 – Space and experience – the future can't just be the topic of a report or presentation. For new generations of decision makers, an experience culture is critical. How can experiences small and large create gateways for understanding possibility?

Chapter 6 – Rules and norms – culture is, in part, a collection of agreed norms and rituals. How can these be harnessed in ways that make thinking about and acting on the future more of a core activity of the organization?

Chapter 7 – Networks and ecosystems – no organization really stands alone. Each is surrounded by ecosystems of partners, supporters, experts, clients, customers or constituents. How can these be harnessed to grow and reinforce a future culture?

Chapter 8 – Conclusion: Maintaining momentum – creating a future culture is only the first step. We finish by looking at ways to keep a culture growing, deepening and thriving on its own.

Chapter 9 – Epilogue: Four futures for future cultures – here, as a short diversion, we look at what the future might hold for the dynamics of future cultures. In particular, we play out some uncertainties around the role of AI in understanding what's next, and whether futuring will be more collaborative or closely held within expert groups.

FIGURE 0.2   Future culture layers

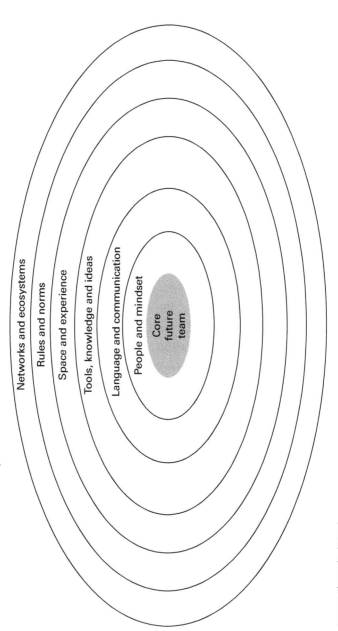

Networks and ecosystems

Rules and norms

Space and experience

Tools, knowledge and ideas

Language and communication

People and mindset

Core
future
team

Source: Changeist (2022)

Appendix – Future cultures resources – finally, we share readings and resources we and our interviewees find valuable in our pursuit of a more anticipatory culture.

Finally, as we did with *How to Future*, we intend to create an online resource around *Future Cultures*, providing supporting tools, additional reading and other content that can help you broaden and deepen your own knowledge and approaches. You can find this at futureculturesbook.com, where we also look forward to receiving your feedback.

A note on terminology

If you come from within the foresight community, you will be aware that a fundamental principle of the future is *plurality*. This is to say that many futurists and those who study the future accept as a given that, at any point in time, many futures are possible. This concept gave rise to the casual use of the plural 'futures' with allied fields of strategic foresight, futures studies and beyond. Nevertheless, usages can and do wander.

As in all of our work, we switch between the singular 'future' to talk about the popular cultural concept, and largely use 'futures' to refer to the broader field of practice or concern, along with 'strategic foresight' to refer to a capacity or discipline. We try to stick to 'futuring' to refer to the ongoing, applied act described and illustrated at the beginning of this introduction.

We hope this word-hopping becomes as natural for you as it has for us over the years. This is in fact a feature, not a bug, as we discuss in Chapter 3.

Let the culture shift begin.

CHAPTER ONE

From function to culture

The future: a question of culture

A workshop participant who had been quietly taking notes and nodding all day, intently focused on our team of instructors and seemingly taking in every word, stood alone by his seat as his colleagues filtered out of the room.

'Thank you, this has been an enjoyable session today, very eye-opening' he said, paraphrasing his polite compliment to our team. 'But, I have a question. All of this is new to me, and I'm learning quite a few new approaches for changing my mindset to be more future-oriented, to think about different future scenarios and what they might mean – this is great.' Then, he paused for a moment. 'But… what do I do when I go back to work later this week?'

'How do you mean?' one of us asked.

'I'm learning all about the value of being more future-minded with my colleagues here, but when I get back to the office, I will be alone. I may have changed *my* views about risk and uncertainty, for example, but I'm the only one. Back at work, things remain the same.'

This particular scene quietly unfolded at the end of the first day of a capacity-building workshop recently, but it wasn't unique. We had heard the same question many times before, phrased in different ways, with slightly different body language, in person and over Zoom. This particular conversation was an encapsulation of many that had come before.

Alone together

In a nutshell, our friend had described the central conflict of our work: how do you develop and maintain an open, agile and anticipatory posture and capability regarding the *future*, while operating successfully in an organization and world that is designed to focus on the *present*? For him, this meant returning to a major global transportation brand where 99.99 per cent of his colleagues are operating in the here and now. In this organization, like the vast majority of businesses, decisions are made on a moment-to-moment basis, driven by everything from real-time global supply costs to weather conditions, to trade relationships, to customer demand. Like the vast majority of organizations, he and his immediate colleagues' and management's compensation are determined not on anticipation of abstract possibilities but on meeting strategic goals, key performance indicators (KPIs) and/or objectives and key results (OKRs) established months or years before.

As we've indicated, our friend is not alone. On occasions too numerous to count, we've been asked – in a quiet corner during lunch break, after a group of stakeholders has cleared the room, or in the safety of a small Zoom gathering – exactly this question. This pattern of asking quietly when few others are around is telling. There's a sense that the questioner has somehow missed an important module or chapter in the textbook. 'Why am I learning these potentially transformative tools if the rest of my organization remains the same?' Surely this isn't intentional, goes the follow-on thought.

The future condition

In truth, this is the condition of modern, applied, professional foresight. In a way similar to other specialist capabilities, such as financial management or industrial design, strategic foresight tends to sit within a single team or unit, often with a very specific label attached to it, like a sign on the door, or titles on a business card. *foresight isn't a* Unlike finance or design, beyond the short- *capability taught* term practice of strategy or executing the *at many schools* latest operating plan, foresight isn't a capability taught at many schools, or a functional professional pathway explored by many people. If you're reading this text, you're probably among a very, very small percentage of the population who actually know a professional futurist or someone who works specifically in a strategic foresight function.

Being few in numbers also means getting lost or sidelined physically in big organizations. When Scott first began working in a formal role as a futurist 20 years ago, nearly every client was a solo futurist or foresight manager sitting inside a global corporation, orbiting somewhere near a corporate strategy office, or relegated to a distant cubicle or building annexe. Our long-running joke at client meetings was that these individual clients were far more like us – their external consultants – than they were like their own corporate colleagues. This extended from our general professional remit down to our comfort with ambiguity and understanding of jargon.

Some big companies have gone as far as making a virtue of the individualism of the futurist. Ford's Sheryl Connolly, a leading figure in corporate futures in the 2000s in the United States,

was frequently cast in the media as 'the' futurist at Ford.[1]
Likewise with Michael Rogers, futurist-in-residence at the *New
York Times* Company, and the iconic David Shing, better known
as Shingy, in his role as 'digital prophet' at AOL.[2] This brief era
of the corporate futurist as rockstar further ensconced the
futures role as a singular, alternative occupation, standing alone
with contrarian ideas, even when these figures were supported
by dedicated teams. But even when well-known in-house futurists do have teams, they are generally segregated from the rest of
the organization, passed from department to department, budget
line to budget line, when reorganizations press bosses to work
out where their most logical home might be.

This difference is something we acknowledge even now. On
successfully guiding a cohort through a futures training course,
we still informally congratulate the graduates on joining a small,
if expanding and diversifying, club. While we don't try to sepa-
rate our charges from their home organizations, we do gently
acknowledge the difference they can feel upon learning new
tools and mindsets. Reflecting on the fundamental shift in her
view of the world, post-course, one participant recently remarked,
'I can't go back to seeing things the same way after this.' Or as
another said, deep into an intensive summer course this past
year, 'I'm enjoying my new eyes!'[3]

Back where we came from

If you've been in professional life for more than a decade, this may
all sound familiar. We have indeed been here before, under the
guise of 'innovation'. This is what lean start-up pioneer Steve Blank
calls 'innovation by exception',[4] that is, when teams are created to
imagine and invent disruptive new products and services, their
capabilities and impacts are intentionally sequestered.

We now see this in futures and foresight, as it was with old-
fashioned research and development before. There used to be an
intentional separation between designated innovators working

on the forward-looking functions of an organization, moving them away from the rest of the body as a way to keep the distractions of new developments and over-the-horizon thinking out of the way of day-to-day execution of necessary tasks. In some cases, it may have even been structured in this way to keep industrial accidents a safe distance from populated corporate buildings or, more metaphorically, to keep potentially dangerous or unsettling ideas about tomorrow distanced from the minds of people paid to execute today's plan.

As Alexandra Deschamps-Sonsino writes in her 2020 book *Creating a Culture of Innovation*, 'A decision about spaces for innovation is, in fact, a decision about power and permissions, two important elements of a culture of innovation.'[5] Who has the power to shape an organization's mission, and who is given the mission to steward? Who is allowed into spaces, be they physical or metaphorical, that catalyse thinking about what may be next, and who defines how to think about it? Physical separation acts as a manifestation of a separation of responsibility and permission, which helps keep the future sealed safely away, a domain that only the different – or superfluous – can enter.

Where does the future fit in a company, team or culture? History points, vigorously, to 'over there,' as if it's an oddly-coloured sofa – that is, useful, but a bit distracting. Futures research, and the people and teams focused on them, too often get separated from the rest of the organization and its ongoing processes, as if putting this function in a hermetically sealed unit makes 'the magic happen', a myth perpetuated by the reverence we give to locations such as the Silicon Valley garages of Apple founder Steve Jobs[6] or Hewlett Packard's David Packard,[7] or MIT's holy of holies, Building 20.[8]

Tense and tensions

To be fair, this struggle with *where* to put the future is a product of the inherent tensions of doing two things at once: running the day-to-day functions of an organization, while keeping an eye on mid- and long-range obstacles or opportunities that are further out on the horizon. There are many such tensions, but a handful come to mind as prominent sources of conflict that keep the future-minded stuck in the middle, so to speak (Figure 1.1):

- **Supporting, but challenging** – futures teams and individuals working in a futures function are expected to stay loyal to the current mission, or follow the current North Star, while simultaneously searching for plausible, supportable reasons to advocate for change. This 'disruption for thee, but not for me' dynamic can keep otherwise insightful people and teams hedging their bets, editing their ideas, or bending them to the current norm.

  futures teams speak differently from their colleagues. As a VP of innovation at a global drinks brand once told a visioning workshop we participated in, 'Remember team, we make fizzy drinks!' Needless to say, this loud reassertion of the current mission in the middle of an open exploration stopped new ideas in their tracks, and probably curtailed participants' willingness to stretch their thinking the next time they engaged with future possibilities. They were being told that any healthy new beverage fitting the lifestyle needs of a health-conscious class of consumers must fit neatly into a cola package. Promoting constraints as 'norms' deeply inhibits futures thinking.

- **Speaking normally, but speaking differently** – futures teams speak differently from their colleagues. While the main body of an organization will speak in terms of products, functions, objectives and measurements, then reinforcing their value through repetition, those working across the room in the futures corner are inventing language to fit new concepts. They are learning and using new terminologies, digesting new grammar, and speaking casually about challenging things like uncertainty and existential risk. Their bread and butter is trafficking in all manner of exotic ideas. A comparative list of a team's Google search terms might give a useful sense of how differently these groups speak, and think.

- **Being a specialist, but also a generalist** – futures teams are expected to be subject-matter experts in all emerging topics, whether it's a particular technological innovation, a fringe phenomenon, a segment of the population or a region of the world, and possibly the intersection of several at the same time. Moreover, they are expected to be the systems thinkers in the organization, connecting the dots and understanding the implications of these connections. They are often relied upon to surface weak signals, follow specialists, absorb research at the pre-peer-review stage, and be linked into unique subcultures. At the same time, they need to demonstrate an in-depth understanding of the company mission, markets and global outlook, and connect new insights back to a current mission.

- **Standing out, but fitting in** – given their area of expertise, or better yet, their time frame of responsibility, futures folks are expected to be a little bit different – aesthetically, temperamentally, and in what they consume, watch and read. From the unusual eyewear (your authors are occasionally guilty here) to a post-modern wardrobe, a direct gaze and demonstrative, TED-like hand gestures, the intention is to be legible as an expert on *tomorrow*. One has to signal strongly that they are living in the present, but sometimes bucking the codes of normality, in order to look the part, as it were. At the same time, they need to demonstrate loyalty to the tribe, trafficking in familiar signifiers, keeping the mission of the organization always in their hearts and minds, and not getting too weird and wild in public, to the point where HR might start getting nervous.

- **Being concrete, while having vision** – so much about modern business, and increasingly government, education and other realms, is data-centric, often dangerously data-philic. Or, what veteran cultural insights strategist John Wise, summarized for us as 'risk averse, data-driven and consensus-driven'.[9] The massive investment in data collection and analysis in many fields over the past decade has made 'evidence-based' a mantra, betting everything on the possibility that absolutely correct decisions can be made on the basis of absolute data. This fixation on ground truth sets up a conflict with exploring what may come next. This was best summarized in 1975 by Ian Wilson, at the time a futurist with GE, when he stated: 'However good our futures research may be, we shall never be able to escape from the ultimate dilemma that all our knowledge is about the past, and all our decisions are about the future.'[10] Yet futures teams are expected to conjure up richly textured visions of the future – at once compellingly exotic, yet commercially viable. Visions should be legible enough to remind the management audience of some future scenario or image they have seen before so as not to estrange, but they should also be creative enough to allow for differentiation.[11]

Stuck in the triangle

These tensions bring to mind the futures triangle, a framework developed by Sohail Inayatullah more than a decade ago in his description of what he sees as the fundamental pillars of futures studies.[12] For Inayatullah, the points of the triangle (see Figure 1.2) are the weight of history, which we can think about as the legacy culture of any organization, the push of the present, in this case the pressure to perform and conform under current market conditions or known contexts, and the pull of the future, or the expectation that futures work will reveal some future that is simultaneously novel and yet recognizable. The centre of this triangle is where the plausible future that is up for discussion rests, sitting in what futurist Alessandro Fergnani refers to as 'contested space'.[13]

What this means in plain language is that owning the job of being 'officially' concerned with the future will always mean being caught in no man's land. To be there is to be stuck between three poles that exert a constantly fluctuating force. In any given moment, is an organization leaning into its heritage, its legacy

FIGURE 1.1 Tensions between the past, present and future faced by future-focused people in organizations

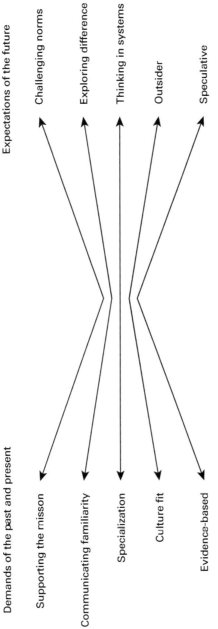

Demands of the past and present

Expectations of the future

Supporting the misson → Challenging norms

Communicating familiarity → Exploring difference

Specialization → Thinking in systems

Culture fit → Outsider

Evidence-based → Speculative

Source: Changeist (2022)

systems, its ways of working, or is it minding the numbers, putting one foot in front of the other, executing on the plan, or is it leaning into its stretch goals, innovating and disrupting its way towards some new North Star?

Aligned with each of these forces are critical resources like funding, staffing and institutional mind-share. Are the powers that be paying attention to you this quarter? Are you a drag keeping the business from living up to its history, are you an unnecessary cost centre scheduled to be axed along with marketing, or are you suddenly the critical tip of the spear, with all bets riding on your insights?

This all sounds terribly dysfunctional, and yet it's the lived experience of just about anyone who has worked in the futures arena on an ongoing basis, ourselves included. A phrase we've long used, 'The future is elastic' sums up our observations of the working environment of organizational futurists over the past few decades. When times are good, the horizons of interest drift gradually further and further out. Organizations can more comfortably dedicate time and resources to investigating the future landscape.

FIGURE 1.2   Futures triangle

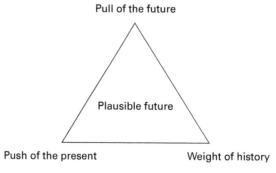

Source: Adapted by Changeist from Inayatullah, S (2008) Six pillars: Futures thinking for transforming, *Foresight*, 10 (1), 4–21

Historically, when a shock hits, or the economic cycle turns downward, counterintuitively, foresight capabilities are one of the first things to get cut from the budget. Because the resources used to support a healthy awareness of the future are usually tucked away inside another department's budget, it's easy to see why this line item can easily be removed. Anecdotally we've seen it happen cycle after cycle over the past two decades.

The outsider view, perceived as being at variance with an organization's main focus, and so valued in more relaxed operating environments, becomes a liability when the time comes to pare down costs and sharpen mission focus in order to ride out turbulence. By enabling such expendability, this historical model of isolating foresight at the edge of an organization, or keeping it small enough to be easily jettisoned, is always short-sighted and rarely effective.

A visionary leader isn't enough

Organizations can't lean exclusively on so-called 'visionary' leaders who make their reputations by being seen by peers and pundits as having an extraordinary capacity for anticipation. The rise of Big Tech over the past few decades, and along with it a media-expert industrial complex that has effectively manufactured the notion of extraordinary people, has fed us the not-so-useful trope of the genius leader who possesses a natural internal foresight.

Doubtless, some have been better at seeing and playing the chess pieces well ahead of others, or, more likely, shaping the chessboard by moving first to define the game others then play. As of this writing in late 2022, however, the news headlines are littered with the downfalls of figures lauded as market prophets the previous year.

Yet, no amount of training, tips or experience can position a single person or even small leadership team to effectively sense the useful environmental signals all the time, make sense of these signals in ways that often cut against the logics and rituals they lead by, and implement them within organizations that are by definition responsive, not anticipatory. Keeping responsibility for active futuring bottled up within the persona of a single leader, or even spread among the inhabitants of the C-suite, is a flawed approach.

Too complex for one person

Not only do these approaches contribute to an unstable environment for all involved and risk putting all an organization's prospective eggs in one fragile basket, they are wholly unsuited for the environment we find ourselves in as we approach the quarter mark of the 21st century – even less so for what is expected to lie ahead. While it's standard operating procedure for any futurist to start out a talk or paper by intoning something like 'We live in a world that's never been more uncertain', living through the past two years has driven this point home to practically everyone who wasn't already among the not insignificant portion of humanity that already lived in daily precarity beforehand.

Whether your go-to acronym to describe the unstable world has been VUCA (volatile, uncertain, complex and ambiguous), a standard since it was introduced by Warren Bennis and Bert Nanus in late 1980s,[14] or the more recently fashionable BANI (brittle, anxious, nonlinear, incomprehensible) coined by futurist Jamais Cascio in 2020,[15] the world is in a state of inherent instability, has been for some time, and looks to continue to be as far ahead on the horizon as we can see.

Regardless of the mapping approach you use, the overall picture is similar. Of the many risks that experts like the World

Economic Forum (WEF) have put on their radars for the past decade, from climate turbulence to infrastructure weaknesses, social unrest, technological failure, resource scarcity and political dysfunction, nearly all are reaching levels of instability, fragility or vulnerability that threaten other critical forces and factors they relate or connect to. As a proxy measure, the World Uncertainty Index, a tool developed by the International Monetary Fund, which uses data mining across the texts of the Economist Intelligence Unit to monitor discussion of uncertainty, has been on a steady climb since 1990, and is currently on another upward spike at the end of 2022.[16]

Economic historian Adam Tooze calls this gestalt phenomenon of entangled risks 'polycrisis', explaining in the *Financial Times*: 'In the polycrisis the shocks are disparate, but they interact so that the whole is even more overwhelming than the sum of the parts.'[17] The resulting uncertainties that emanate from these interconnected risks create an environment rife with signals of change, but one that is also harder to effectively make sense of in a strategic context. The subtle or even invisible linkages among different forces and factors suddenly become visible – often painfully so – leaving the typical leader, hyperfocused on execution of the latest strategic plan, flat-footed and scrambling for expertise and insight. What looked like a straightforward chart of inputs and outputs becomes a tangled map of interlocking vulnerabilities.

It's no longer the case that you have to be in a volatile market like finance or energy to experience the sideswipe of an unexpected force changing the landscape in front of you in an instant. Whether you're a software developer, schoolteacher, dishwasher, parent, copywriter, parliamentarian, tea grower, welder or aid worker, you have already experienced some aspect of polycrisis in the echoing impacts of a local virus outbreak turned global pandemic. Risks become less about 'either/or' situations, and more about chains of 'and'. Uncertainty levels spike, and decision making becomes far more complex. And, to add to the challenge, what may look at one moment like a risk may be turned by another organization or actor in the system into an opportunity in the next moment, creating an environment where the pathway towards a preferable future is constantly shifting.

In our professional view, this state of polycrisis isn't going to resolve itself in a cyclic fashion in the foreseeable future, though it may ebb and flow. For example, we've seen measures taken to mitigate recent major supply chain disruptions triggered by the pandemic have some effect, and many products are flowing again along globalized channels for the moment. Yet, the Covid-19 pandemic was only an impact of several larger forces intersecting – climate change, urbanization and globalization among them, each of which continues.

Climate change itself is happening in the most complex system we know, across which perturbations are rippling with greater frequency as global warming increases, triggering many other uncertainties, including economic, social, political and technological ones. Impacts and interventions across this web of forces also present unique new opportunities, whether from a technological innovation, change in social values, emergence of new political or economic models or some wholly unanticipated outcome. From the crucible of heightened risk and uncertainty new, sustainable, equitable ways of living, working, travelling, learning, feeding and clothing ourselves, etc, can emerge. In short, everything is in play.

MOVING BEYOND THE MOONSHOT MINDSET

For the better part of the 2010s until quite recently, the moonshot metaphor has been a popular way to conceptualize the future, particularly if you are an American and somehow tied to the technology sector. The popularization of the idea, which borrowed from the challenging, expensive and high-profile push to land a human on the moon in the 1960s, has also carried it into UK innovation strategy, European Union R&D, Japanese innovation[18] and academia, as innovation research Olivier Usher has described.[19] We've seen moonshots in everything from vaccines and cancer research to semiconductors and ageing.

Google was so enamoured of the moonshot metaphor that, in 2010, it spun off a unit it called X, The Moonshot Factory, to work on complex big bets, going even further than competitors Amazon and Meta. Though in early 2023, it seems they have all radically scaled their moonshot projects back after years of flooding them with cheap money, staff and big ambitions.[20] Nevertheless, in their time, moonshots became a kind of shiny cultural object, attracting attention, headlines, fawning analysis and not a little envy, from corporate managers and politicians alike.

One side effect of all this excitement has been the way it has reframed futures discourse in this time, raising expectation among leaders and managers that futures work should be a 'go big or go home' endeavour, applied for the purposes of yielding blockbuster outcomes, or, in other cases, saving the institutional bacon. The overselling of disruption and transformation as a primary product of futures work by high-profile practitioners hasn't helped.

Positioning a futures team to principally be a vending machine for breakthrough ideas is self-defeating, both in terms of the perceived efficacy of that team over time, and the narrow scope of exploration this implies. While it may generate opportunities for lovely graphics and TED-like talks, it vastly underutilizes the wider spectrum of value that futuring can provide as a platform for early sensing, critical sense-making and strategic discussion.

A key challenge, then, of establishing an enduring future culture is getting past the moonshot mentality among organizational leadership that only big leaps are possible or desirable. Even though the challenges many organizations and certainly many societies face are enormous, complex and ever evolving, there is absolutely a place for smaller-scale, less sexy, but necessary 'roofshots', as Google fellow Luiz André Barroso once termed the moonshot alternative,[21] that is, smaller innovations, course adjustments or other quick wins that achieve the valuable 'hops' from the tenuous present towards a more preferable future, step by step, and manageably.

Activating the whole of the organization

We lay out these conditions, both the general historical context of consulting futurists within an organization and the turbulent map of risks and opportunities, to point to a simple reality: it no longer makes sense to rely on just a small part of any organization to carry the weight of anticipating the future. The core of this work may still reside functionally with a few individuals or teams, but it must be connected to, fed by, informed and activated throughout the rest of the entity, and even the ecosystem that supports it. *Every person should be connected to the future culture of an organization, and considered a critical contributor to and participant in that culture, no matter their role.*

Every person should be connected to the future culture of an organization, no matter their role.

What we described in *How to Future* as 'futuring', choosing the verb form intentionally to denote constant action, is something that must become part of the DNA of every organization that hopes to survive and thrive in the coming years. Futuring must become integral to the nature of the organization – not simply an expressed value, buzzword or aspiration, but as part of its ongoing state of thinking, doing and being, and invested in by the people that inhabit it.

In his 1973 work *The Interpretation of Cultures*, anthropologist Clifford Geertz described culture 'not as complexes of concrete behavior patterns – customs, usages, traditions, habit clusters – as has, by and large, been the case up to now, but as a set of control mechanisms – plans, recipes, rules, instructions (what computer engineers call 'programs') – for the governing of behavior.'[22] In the face of so much interlocking change, it would seem almost quaint to say today that organizations need to change their habits and traditions, but perhaps insufficiently humanistic to argue for a change in programming.

Given that so much of our daily lives are a blend of ritual and code, we're arguing for a mixture of these two ends of the spectrum – that futuring needs to become part of both the ingrained ritual, habit and norms of an organization at a social level, and through that, woven into the rule sets and code by which it runs at an operational one. After all, the way organizations operate is just that – an encoded set of practices and rituals believed to be of benefit to that organization as a collective culture, in context of the role and mission of that organization. Making a group, team or organization more future-oriented requires reprogramming the culture gradually, but steadily, by inviting it and encouraging it to shift practices, rituals and ways of communication through and about these.

Building the culture from the inside out

As much as we identify it with external representation such as forecasts, images, narratives, models, diagrams and other artefacts, the act of foresight very much begins as an internal construct. There is no fixed, universal model of what constitutes the future inside our heads, but many different understandings.

Each of us conceptualizes the future in different ways, shaped by our wider culture, our learning throughout life, our biases and our personal experiences, and develops the capacity for foresight based on these and many other factors.

As a subjective practice, no one arrives at a job in an organization with the single certified model of the future and accompanying process for the exercise of foresight. Despite many of us sharing some common ideas or beliefs about the future, and maybe having the same understanding of some formal approaches and methodologies, there is no fixed common concept to work from. In a 2004 paper, organizational researchers Deborah A Blackman and Steven Henderson put it succinctly: 'Foresight is merely a picture, a mental model to guide decisions and actions operating between the present and the expected future state.'[23]

Building a culture of futuring, then, starts with the individual and their mindset – the sum of their experiences, beliefs, assumptions, interests, capabilities, dispositions towards change and uncertainty, and how they exercise these. How these are expressed, framed, and acted upon is where foresight begins in any organization – what a person or people do with what they believe, discover and determine. This is where we start in the next chapter, looking at the importance of people and mindsets as the keystone of a future culture, before journeying further to look at the expressions, places, platforms, norms and networks that form the scaffolding of this culture.

DISTINGUISHING RISK FROM UNCERTAINTY

In his 2020 book *The Uncertainty Mindset*, Vaughn Tan, assistant professor at University College London's School of Management, provides a useful and succinct way to think about certainty, risk, and true uncertainty. Of the first category, he writes, 'In a certain world, you have all the knowledge necessary to know exactly how

---

the future will be.'[24] Here, all needed information is available about both past and possible futures, leaving no space for doubt or ambiguity. This, of course, is vanishingly rare.

As for risk, Tan frames it in terms of measurability. 'The word risk here means that the exact future that will result is unknown, but the different possible futures are knowable in a way that allows you to plan by calculating how likely different possible futures are and taking clearly sensible actions based on those calculations. To be clear, this requires a type of certainty about the unknowns…'[25] This, by the way, is the category today's leaders try valiantly to model, using historical data and predictive analytics, and then financialize, by finding ways to hedge risk. However, the data is only as good as the assumptions made in modelling it, and those assumptions require some certainty about the way the world will continue to work.

Finally, of the third category, Tan writes: 'True uncertainty is a different form of uncertainty that cannot be measured and cannot be eliminated using strategies chosen based on likelihoods of outcomes.'[26] Giving an example of a company in a situation of true uncertainty, Tan continues: 'Your company's exact future is unknown, but you know neither all of the possible futures nor how likely each of those possible futures is. You aren't able to calculate how likely the different possible futures are… and make sensible decisions about what you should do based on such calculations.'[27]

In a world of cascading discontinuities, where customers, partners, adversaries or markets can and do behave in counterintuitive ways, more and more organizations find themselves operating in a landscape of true uncertainty.

CHAPTER TWO

People and mindset

JOB TITLE   Senior Futurist

Are you looking to shape tomorrow? Are you keen to spot the future before it arrives? Do you see yourself as an evangelist for change? We are looking for a new senior futurist to anchor a growing team dedicated to looking out for what's next. We seek an early career professional with a unique mix of left- and right-brain thinking, highly tuned quantitative and qualitative expertise, an in-depth knowledge of statistics, engineering, sociology and policy, and world-class communication skills.

You'll be asked to:

- Research new trends and develop horizon-scanning capabilities
- Provide in-depth analysis of emerging issues and highly accurate forecasts that predict what's next
- Feed the innovation pipeline with high potential leads
- Develop new reports and studies and deliver presentations

- Design and facilitate workshops
- Advise senior executives on critical decision making
- Recruit and hire a team of junior futurists
- Manage public communications about the future

Salary range: N/A

People and mindset: the culture embodied

Within months of Covid's outbreak, foresight-related roles were popping up in the jobs section of LinkedIn like mushrooms after a rain. Not all were like the fictional ad above, but many did (and still do) ask for the moon, throwing many different and conflicting qualifications into one bucket, looking for a rare mix of people to effectively absorb organizational risk.

Adding to this, even in 'normal' times, by comparison with other functions and departments, there is usually very little integration between a futures team and the body of the wider organization, and this push to expand capacity in some ways exacerbates the problem. Many employees won't be aware of what this team does, or what insights they produce, and even the C-suite may generally ignore their work in favour of the immediate needs of the present.

This is why investing in a company-wide future culture is so important for building a successful futures-focused organization. Not everyone has to be a full-time futurist, but enabling colleagues to feel more comfortable thinking about uncertainty and possibility is very valuable. Teaching them the language and supporting their efforts to apply futures approaches is even more so.

If the pandemic taught us anything, being prepared for unexpected situations might be top of mind for a majority of individuals and organizations today. Having a contingency plan, understanding the impacts of a decision, or anticipating unintended consequences are all skills more of us have developed over the past few years. In other words, more and more people are activating their capacity for anticipation, but much of it remains unfocused, like the job ad above.

Just to clarify, futurists don't *predict* the future. We see our practice as a way to help organizations understand the landscape of possible futures, then make decisions based on that landscape as it may look, 5, 10, even 25 years on. Tactical and strategic decisions *futurists don't* can be made to provide resilience in a reasonable *predict the* number of future scenarios. The idea is not to get *future.* one future that's absolutely right, but several possible futures that serve to guide towards preferable futures for the constituents that matter. This may sound arduous, but as more people contribute, the process becomes more comprehensive and resilient.

Niklas Larsen, Senior Advisor at the Copenhagen Institute for Futures Studies explains that, 'The better humans can become at understanding different explanations of and methods for imagining the future, the less reason there will be to fear the future, and the better they will be able to harness future opportunities and make sense of change and novelty.'[1] By including those in the broader body of the organization, many will develop new insight into the work they are doing for today, which makes products, services or policies more resilient in the face of the types of turbulence or possibility we describe in the Introduction.

It starts with people

When we teach our How to Future courses, there will always be a couple of people in each cohort who have an Archimedes *Eureka!* moment. Their eyes light up and they nod along and are very excited to know more about the tools and processes we teach. But that doesn't mean that the rest of a cohort aren't equally immersed in learning about futures mindsets, tools and methods.

As we describe in Chapter 1, building a future culture doesn't mean hiring a clutch of academics from futures studies programmes and sequestering them in some far-off corner and hoping their work will catch on (or not). Our experience has shown us over and over that far more people have a natural tendency to notice indicators of change and make sense of them, but 99 per cent of them aren't invited into futuring activities in any meaningful way.

These days, very few corporate or government practitioners have an academic background in futures, having mostly learnt on the job from senior staff on their teams, though more and more are investing in some form of basic capacity building in the futures realm, as evidenced by the explosion of futures education offerings globally, including everything from lengthy technical courses to short, bite-sized introductions for casual learners.

We've been working in this area of futures education for over a decade, preceding even our work with Changeist, and have seen the growth of the market first-hand. There is a breadth of demand for these programmes, from seasoned senior professionals to secondary-school-aged learners, and a full spectrum of ways to deliver the essential elements – the latter accelerated by hybrid working requirements of the last few years.

Finding future-ready people

Those who can anticipate change and express how change may impact the future have a heightened instinct for making better tactical and strategic decisions. We've started thinking of people who fit this description as 'high anticipatory potential individuals', or HAPIs for short. The first step in building a future culture is finding the people who can best model the mindset. People come first. An organization with a strong future culture will develop a network of people throughout who can communicate across departmental lines, weaving soft networks with like-minded colleagues as they go.

HAPI TRAITS

When setting out to establish a future culture within an organization, these are some traits to look for when building an internal capability from scratch, or knitting together a network:

- **Curious** – people who exhibit a heightened ability to notice change can become the seeds for establishing a more deeply-rooted future culture. Seeking information about the wider world, or even just outside the responsibilities of work – being curious – is an excellent trait to look for in futures-oriented thinkers. This ability should be cultivated and encouraged.

    Cheryl Chung, Head of Singapore at Kantar Public, expressed that her most important interview question is, 'What do you read?' She shared that this question gives her a much better understanding of a potential employee than a CV filled with impressive degrees and job titles. Look for people who want to understand how the world works, how its decision makers think, and what others experience. Seek out those who take in information from both confirming and contradictory sources, with wide-ranging views and an understanding of bias. Curiosity is the gateway to understanding systems and their dynamics.[2]

- **Aware** – the best scanners have a wider view of the world, and cultivate a habit of picking up new information. They perhaps even read information in their ambient environment with more of a future-focused lens, so they become adept at what we defined in *How to Future* as 'active noticing', that is continuously and constructively sensing information in the world around themselves. 'Active noticers may be good primary generators of observations, but they're also good consumers of other people's perceptions,'[3] we wrote, describing how this engagement with the world can kick-start a virtuous cycle of both awareness and contribution.

This doesn't necessarily mean only those who are highly educated or well-travelled. Seeking out people who have interesting hobbies, who know sports stats for their favourite team, have emigrated, or lived in another culture, have changed careers, or those who come from an underrepresented minority can often make excellent scanners as they are already attuned to noticing 'What's different here?' The latter category often have much more highly tuned risk awareness than those who live in comfortable, insulated worlds.

John Carney, Principal Synthesist within the Futures Innovation Group at the Defence Science and Technology Laboratory (DSTL) explains how important people are to this process, saying: 'Horizon Scanning has resourcing implications as it is a people intensive activity since human beings are required to draw out connections and the implications of findings – an essentially creative process that cannot yet be automated.'[4] The more people who come to the organization with these inclinations and habits, the wider and more diverse the eventual sensing network of the organization can become.

· **Open-minded** – a Google Doc full of links to 'signals' is not of much use until shared and socialized by people who can offer diverse perspectives on what a particular signal might mean. After all, many futures methods were designed specifically to draw out and analyse varying assumptions and perspectives. Encouraging insight sharpening through engaging people who have an openness to exchanging ideas can build a stronger future culture and provide fresh insights to make an organization better at anticipating change. Philip Tetlock, Wharton professor and co-author of *Superforecasting: The art and science of prediction* rates open-mindedness to new information as one of the top traits of high-quality forecasters.[5]

It's worth noting, particularly in these times of increased social stress and contention, that what we suggest looking for, and encouraging, are people who have a natural inclination for discovery, of which the willingness to engage in useful, respectful discussion and unpacking of ideas is part – what one futures colleague at a major car manufacturer calls being a 'polite contrarian'. We aren't talking necessarily about people who relish an intellectual sparring match just for the sake of argument, or to raise their own profile. Social media provides enough of that today. Futuring isn't a zero-sum game of absolute knowledge. Respect for perspectives and a safe space for exchange are crucial to its success.

- **Adaptable** – keeping an open mind, taking on new information and being willing to consider other points of view is a deeply important and increasingly hard to find characteristic. Being adaptable doesn't mean being wishy-washy or non-committal, it means being able to think things through and consider new information and potentially change one's mind, find a new perspective or discover a new approach to a problem. The most naturally anticipatory people are often those who take on new perspectives and learn from others' insights, recalibrating and refining their own along the way.

Those who are adaptable are the Swiss army knives that make a futures network stronger.

Adaptability can also mean being able to bring different disciplinary skills to problem framing or solving. The best futures teams we've seen in the field are those that mix educational and vocational backgrounds, blending people with backgrounds in the arts and humanities with those who have trained in the sciences, for example. Our own extended team brings together people with background or experience in everything from design research to market research to graphic design and art direction to literature and play, and we often find ourselves reaching across disciplinary boundaries for approaches or ideas to create a fresh point of view.

Colleagues of Jeanette Kwek, Head of the Centre for Strategic Futures (CSF) in Singapore often refer to her as a 'Swiss army knife'. It's an apt description of her many skills, and a useful metaphor for who to look for when building a futures network within a team or organization. Those who are adaptable are the Swiss army knives that make a futures network stronger.[6]

- **Entrepreneurial** – several of the futures leaders we spoke to for this book identified an entrepreneurial nature as being among the qualities that make good leaders in a futuring culture, particularly in its early stages. People taking initiative is a common theme through many of our discussions, and rings true with our own experience. As a group that is often pushed to the fringes within their organization – maybe they are not well resourced or staffed, or are generally perceived as being 'experimental' – means that having people who are willing to take the lead in thinking, identifying sources of support, connecting others, exploring unknown terrain, being able to scope tasks without direction, and looking for new opportunities to leverage futuring is tremendously valuable. Such people can have enough conviction about their work to keep at it, despite obstacles they may encounter.

- **Empathetic** – in a world of cold, dispassionate data and measurable outcomes, having an understanding of the breadth of the human condition can be highly valuable in futuring. Only bringing one's privileged view, or just a probabilistic lens to possible futures is limiting at best, and detrimental at worst. Being able to change seats, metaphorically, and look at indicators and signals through other eyes can bring greater depth, not just to individual capacity for anticipation, but to overall future culture. This perspective-taking means being able to think about how a particular future might feel to others. While we can't have perfect empathy, and should take care considering the lived experiences of others, at a minimum, it means being able to see beyond our own experience.

- **Comfortable with uncertainty** – uncertainty is defined as situations that involve imperfect or unknown information, and for most people this can be a stumbling block for decision making, even at the most basic level. People who can approach uncertainty with discernment for potential risks and opportunities are able to more effectively move beyond present-day constraints to imagine more robust outcomes in the future.

   As Vaughn Tan writes, some people develop a greater capacity for operating under uncertainty, perhaps having worked in environments where resources are in flux, conditions ambiguous and failure a real possibility. Ironically, Tan's research is not into high-stakes finance or special ops, but new restaurant development![7] Those who are comfortable with uncertainty often have a healthy relationship with risk, neither seeking it out nor hiding from it, or trying to over-control it. The first set of conditions describes much of the world today, but the latter characteristic narrows the population down significantly.

   This comfort with uncertainty extends beyond situations, to information. If, as the saying goes, there are no facts about the future, being comfortable with fuzzy or incomplete information, and being able to orient oneself in a field of unclear indicators is also desirable. This comfort can be a precursor to an ability to make sense and develop maps through uncertainty.

- **Attuned to impacts** – an ability to describe impacts, or implications of change over time, is one of the most valuable traits on this list. Describing a trend, then tracing a linear path of 'Then what?' and 'What comes next?' takes a futuring mindset to a higher level. This is not an ability to move from problem to solution in a straight line, but rather a wide-angle exploration of many possible impacts, positive or negative, and how they might resolve over time. With practice, probing impacts can become a natural habit and a great practice to engage in across a future culture.

- **Systems thinker** – we point to this above, but it's worth saying clearly: futuring is all about considering complexity and the many interactions within a system or systems, rather than reducing things to simplest terms or making insider predictions. Some backgrounds and disciplines lend themselves to considering systemic behaviours, and we've seen people with strong futuring capabilities come from fields as diverse as urban planning and marine biology.

Whether hiring, nominating or identifying people within an organization to be involved with futuring activities, or looking for sponsors and advocates who will help build a network, these traits are an excellent starting place for building a future culture. Encouraging networks of these types within teams or divisions helps strengthen opportunities for shared insights and stronger consensus in decision making. Finding people with all of these qualities can be challenging at first, but the more defined the future culture becomes, the more such people may self-identify.

LOOKING FOR THE 'OUTSIDE' VIEW, OR POLITICAL INSIGHT?

An 'outside' view is generally understood to refer to psychologist Daniel Kahneman's and business strategist Dan Lovallo's widely accepted interpretation of seeking a wide range of examples from similar situations to improve decision making. Rather than building only from a single case, there is value in people who seek relevant information about analogous or adjacent situations to provide a more comprehensive perspective and bring new information to the table for more vigorous debate. This is where it can be valuable to find people who have honed some of the personal attributes above in a different sector, and who can apply similar patterns more than similar cases to a challenge or question.

Many of the experts we spoke with stressed the importance of understanding organizational politics as well. This doesn't have to mean the exact politics of the organization they've joined, but having an appreciation for how decisions are made by people in power can help navigate the tricky dynamics of building future culture to include senior decision makers.

Most of all, this calls for good culture builders to be good observers, to look for patterns and understand systems broadly – being able to read the landscape. Situations may change, but often the terrain remains constant.

Other kinds of diversity: building future-diverse teams

There is no single correct way to create an internal network focused on futures, but one important element is aiming for diversity – of thought, skills, education, life experience, as well as gender and ethnic identity. This isn't always easy, but it can be useful to keep in mind that the more widely diverse a team is, the better it can imagine futures that recognize the needs of a broader range of stakeholders in that future.

No team will ever be perfectly balanced in diversity, so it's useful to seek out people who are aware of their own cultural norms and beliefs and how that may influence bias in their thinking. It also helps, if groups that are less diverse out of necessity or through entrenched hiring practices, that it is possible to mitigate negative consequences for others by acknowledging this in advance of any project. An audience or user should never be constrained to seeing scenarios that only represent the needs of the team itself.

EXAMINING BIASES

Divergence of thought, debate and even outright disagreement are vital to providing rigour to futures work. Being able to ask the right questions and engaging in vigorous conversation helps pull out a fuller range of possibilities. Respectful debate helps teams do higher-quality work. Everyone comes to the table with their own level of understanding, competencies, subject-matter expertise, mental models and views of how the world works. Asking questions leads to high standards of proof, which leads to more robust results.

Teams needn't be static and should change over time. There's great value in assembling teams based on the questions at hand, or to get a different balance of skills based on a different approach. Some teams may never really gel, but that's OK. The highest quality of work usually comes from teams with an unexpected mix of skills, experiences and points of view.

HIRING FOR USEFUL SKILLS, NOT SAFE ONES

We often see 'futurist' positions posted on LinkedIn and other job sites that call for a wide array of skills that are either superfluous or oddly misguided in terms of the work. MBAs, data analysts, statisticians and engineers, while often innovative, are not automatically well-suited for work that requires finding possibility within a landscape of unknown unknowns. This is not to say that those who work in these areas aren't capable of embracing future culture practices, it's just to say that those who can are rare gems who should be encouraged to participate in an internal futures network.

While it may not be immediately possible to begin adding the traits described above to job descriptions, it is worth approaching HR to include language that suggests these traits are 'nice to haves' when posting for new positions within a team or organization. Those in charge of staffing may not be familiar with the nature of the work, which is where such a discussion can be useful. Revising job descriptions to reflect an investment in a future culture also helps to reframe 'culture fit' as a new dynamic for modern hiring practices.

CULTURE CATALYST   Finding your people

It can be hard enough to hire today, but to recruit for what are really tacit qualities can be challenging. While you can check qualifications during an interview process, it may take a little longer to get a sense of teammates' softer skills and qualities. After all, anyone can say they are curious or open-minded, but how do they respond in real-time situations?

Also, not everyone walks in the door futuring-ready, as much as they may express excitement or enthusiasm for what they *think* the task may be. There are far, far more people we would call *future-philic*, that is, those who think the future is cool or interesting more than they might naturally fit into a futuring team. A simple enthusiasm or subject-matter interest in a certain area, such as technology, can in some ways work against the need for objective open-mindedness.

- **Mapping the team** – one simple approach to getting a sense of who exhibits which strengths over time may be to use something like the map in Figure 2.1 to gauge how strongly a person exhibits the various HAPI characteristics we list above. Is someone particularly strong in most categories? They may make a good candidate to recruit into an expanding futures team right away. Are they strong in some, but less so in others? Could you find ways to help the person in question sharpen these weaker skills, or pair them with someone who exhibits that strength? Without a way to assess the qualities of both existing teammates and potential hires, you may be left with a patched-together team assigned by HR due to technical skills, but lacking in the softer sense-making skills that really power this work.

- **Weaving the network** – some of the professionals we interviewed for this book stressed the importance of smart sponsors and stakeholders who *get it*. 'They're big readers, they're very curious… they're seeing all these things', Joanna Lepore, Global Foresight Director for McDonald's, remarked to us. '[Good sponsors] have a natural inclination to be passionate about [the future]. They just get foresight.' Often you find these things out in the midst of a project, or you may have been approaching a possible sponsor or supporter internally who just doesn't align with your team. If you have the opportunity and time to identify your *possible* network – your natural allies and supporters – this just might help you map out which directions to build out your culture, and see who has qualities aligned with your team. You can also do this by running the same exercise as described above, but overlay it on an organizational chart to get a sense of where your most natural paths of support may lie (Figure 2.2).[8]

FIGURE 2.1   Team assessment map

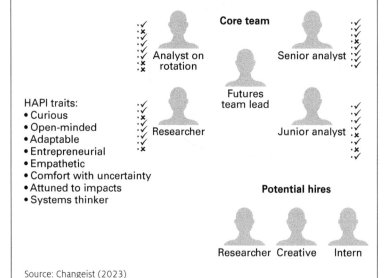

Source: Changeist (2023)

FIGURE 2.2   Organizational assessment map

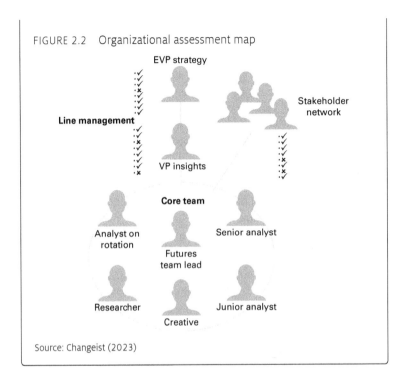

Source: Changeist (2023)

FINDING FERAL FUTURISTS

It's not uncommon today to find a handful of people in an organization that self-define as futurists, distinct from their actual job titles. The trend towards informality in titles and functional labels at work, along with the desire to signal to like-minded people outside the organization have both fed this phenomenon. A cursory browse of LinkedIn or Twitter will turn up #futurist in descriptors for a range of people who either take it into their own hands to keep up with new trends, those who may dabble informally in foresight, advocate for change in their business or industry, or who just identify with what they might call 'futurism'.

So, what do you do with these folks, as someone charged with building a futuring culture?

- **Find them** – this may include running a search on social networks for people in your organization using a few keywords, putting out the word on internal chat, or even running an event or webinar that encourages future-minded folks to find you. If doing the latter, know that there is a kind of self-identification curve. A lot of people may sign up for something they think is going to give them some new insight or data about what's next, but may not self-identify as a futurist per se. Find some way to help them find you.

- **Collect them** – find opportunities to learn more about how they self-identify. Who would like to be better at futuring versus who is simply a fan of innovation? Everyone can be engaged, but this may help sort people by interest.

- **Connect them** – now you've identified a few people, how can you keep them together? The IBM example below shows one way to create venues for people to express their interest, share their knowledge and learn more about a future culture approach. Book clubs, short workshops, even quick brainstorming sprints can help bring people together. Solicit ideas about interesting activities, reading, speakers or other ideas that can provide glue to the connection.

- **Align them** – once you've connected them, this is a good opportunity to discuss the common vocabulary you want to share as an internal culture. How do you talk about trends, or scenarios, or horizons? What common definitions can you use collectively to be on the same page? What, if anything, is the current organizational point of view on big future topics? What projects may be going on that people can contribute to, which help them build the futuring culture?

According to Mick Costigan, VP of Salesforce Futures at Salesforce, the global cloud software company that has its own core futures team led by Chief Futures Officer Peter Schwartz – an early proponent of scenario planning – his group are not the only future-focused people among the firm's 70,000-plus employees.

'There are quite a few people across Salesforce with approximations of the word futurist in their title,' he told us. 'Some came in with acquisitions and continue to play an important role in aspects of future strategy and content development for those business units. Others are part of our "evangelist team" and have a significant role engaging with different parts of the customer or tech analyst community, which is often where they came from. They participate in conferences, engage with analysts and advise customers' he said.[9]

Asked how the two cultures – expert and interested – blend, Costigan said the two successfully interrelate. 'We find that people are excited about the fact that the company has a futures team that does this kind of work, and that we're interested in their opinions. We do find that questions that relate to the company's values do particularly interest those employees when we ask for their input.'[10]

Connecting the rest: helping mixed cultures succeed

In their book *Superforecasting*, Philip Tetlock and Daniel Gardner use Archilochus' fable of 'The Hedgehog and the Fox' to explain ways of thinking about the world. Tetlock describes those who are better at forecasting in general as 'foxes' because they can hold multiple points of view and adapt as they learn over time. 'Foxes have different strategies for different problems. They are comfortable with nuance, they can live with contradictions. Hedgehogs, on the other hand, focus on the big picture. They reduce every problem to one organizing principle.'[11]

What can be useful in developing a future culture is bringing foxes and hedgehogs together to consider specific questions as they arise. Discussing the optimum mix for a futuring team, strategist John Wise described his ideal using just that analogy: 'Somebody who lives in fox mindset but can speak hedgehog language, I think is a really powerful person.' For Wise, this means looking for a set of situational skills – able to navigate uncertainty themselves, but also able to translate their findings or insights into a legible point of view. Foxes and hedgehogs can work together on tough problems by using language that resonates with those who have a harder time finding nuance, or are uncomfortable with uncertainty.[12]

Having inclusive conversations with those who find futures thinking challenging can often lead to much more robust positions on the questions being explored. The idea is not to exclude hedgehogs, but to utilize their subject-matter expertise to more concretely understand particular constraints or frameworks that must be acknowledged to arrive at an informed point of view.

Paul Fein, writing for the Association for Talent Development puts it this way: 'The future-focused organization must have a culture based on balancing behavioral expectations of all employees – freedom versus focused discipline, collaboration versus independence, experimenting openly versus structured exploration, non-confrontational versus strong honesty, individual accountability versus team connections.'[13]

An ability to seek out the right people for any futures-focused project starts with approaching potential collaborators with an understanding of the abilities and skills they bring to the table. These can be internal or external to the organization, as necessary. The next step is to invite them into a network of other subject-matter experts who are relevant to the topic, plus some generalists, along with futurists or foresight strategists, to form an ad hoc team for exploring possibilities. These networks can be formal or informal, long or short term, as no two projects will be exactly the same.

Convening communities

Creating a network within an organization that talks to each other, sharing signals they have found, or meeting together to discuss topics of interest, and having conversations about what X means in Y world, opens up vast opportunities for new insights and points of view that may shape or shift what products, services or policies are being designed in the present. Expanding participation in future-oriented discussions builds resilience and affords people a chance to contribute in ways that perhaps aren't possible within their own team or division.

Creating a network within an organization opens up vast opportunities for new insights

For example, IBM invests heavily in an internal culture that supports teams and networks across the organization (see Chapter 6 for more on IBM's futuring journey). It calls this 'Garage culture', which is described as 'collaboration across roles, focus on business instead of departmental objectives, trust, and value placed on learning through experimentation'.[14]

EXAMPLE

In 2021, a group of three IBM employees started a company-wide 'guild' focused on strategic foresight and the allied field of speculative design. Guilds, a formally used term at Big Blue, are 'Autonomous squads... of diverse squad members who have a wide variety of skills.'[15]

When discussing his team's creation of the Strategic Foresight Guild, Dan Silveira, a service and experience design consultant in the company's Toronto office noted, 'IBM is known for having many different types of guilds that each focus on a different area of practice. It really becomes a way to centralize the practice within the company, and then allow people to learn from there.'

The initial intention of the guild was to create a central space where those who were passionate about innovation could collaborate and learn from one another, developing a culture and community within IBM around strategic foresight.[16]

Silveira continued by expressing how deliberate they were in offering a variety of ways to interact and participate in the Guild. They decided to facilitate three different types of sessions, lecture or talk, workshop, or a sharing session. This makes it possible for any guild members to participate, express themselves, or share their thinking in venues in which they feel most comfortable. Executive buy-in was also vitally important and helped the Guild to grow quickly.[17]

Now that remote and hybrid work have become a norm, it can be challenging for a fledgling futures network to grow and flourish. Since 2020 we have worked with several organizations to build an internal platform for signal scanning and trend development that form the kernel of a wider futuring network, as it acts not just as a knowledge management tool, but as a proxy space for sharing and discovering (see more in Chapter 4). These platforms offer a unique opportunity for building a set of social practices and futuring culture around the insights they contain, which can be particularly valuable for organizations that are large and dispersed, where convening over the coffee machine or sharing the same sofa isn't practical.

Encouraging people to contribute to an online platform, and providing training in best practices in submitting and formatting signals helps encourage foresight capacity building while at the same time providing upskilling to support employees in their careers. We've found that investment in these sorts of collaborative platforms demonstrates valuable returns at both organizational and individual levels.

Essentially, getting buy-in for building a future culture can be top-down, or bottom-up. What's important is understanding organizational culture and finding and speaking to an audience that will be receptive to new ways of thinking and new tools that will support their day-to-day work.

CASE STUDY Futuring in government

Over the years, we've had multiple opportunities to work with governments or individual government departments and engage in futures and foresight work with them. We've also consulted with many government divisions that have their own internal foresight teams. Futures work for a government is different, and somewhat unique, but some of the best futures people we know work in government, specifically from Dubai, Singapore and the UK.

In speaking with these practitioners about their day-to-day work we realized that there were many commonalities among the tools and methods they use, as well as their ways of communicating with audiences to present trends, scenarios and narratives, and assisting their non-futurist colleagues when designing policymaking, services or infrastructure projects, so they might be more resilient over time. This is challenging work and can be especially difficult when evidence is held as the main currency on which people who govern rely to do the work their citizens will benefit from.

Sadly, with no hard data about the future (never heartening for a civil servant or bureaucrat to hear), futurists in government service are tasked with a huge responsibility to consider all the right questions and then propose the best approaches for any potential catastrophe, or opportunity, they might surface, because even the smallest missteps can have huge consequences for a government.

Politics can make it challenging to raise negative possibilities because then plans will have to be made for that eventuality, and governments have to be delicate about discussing possible impacts of pandemics, or climate change, or financial collapse. Thus, government foresight work is a tightrope walk, but that's what makes many futurists who work in government so good at what they do.

Dr Noah Raford, the former Futurist-in-Chief for the Dubai Government and founding executive of the Dubai Future Foundation, speaks about the ebb and flow of futures work in government, where one day everything is about preparing for the next crisis, but as a current crisis recedes and the mood improves, the next is all about finding new opportunities. He finds that foresight in a government context is sometimes 'about trying to get some kind of reassurance or comfort, or to use an output as a persuasive tool to shape whatever decision [an entity] wants to make.'[18]

Raford speaks of crises as being an opportunity for futures leadership to enter the 'public managerial mind' because it offers a 'magical window of awareness that the world doesn't always work the way we think it works'. Once embedded, a futures team can shift towards helping government entities deliver their mission through a more visionary, rather than reactionary, lens. This offers the added benefit of encouraging everyone in those entities to think about the future more effectively as part of their daily duties as well.[19]

Raford suggests that it's vitally important for a futures team to always reframe long-term potentials as actionable projects that an organization can work on now, in the present. Internal futures teams need to be able to translate their long-term insights and provide clear evidence as to their recognizable organizational value right now. An organization that invests in a future culture makes enumerating that value a more streamlined process because the institution itself understands the value of futures work.

Like Dubai, Singapore is also a place where the future is always top of mind. Singapore puts a strong government focus on its future and invests heavily in building a strong internal foresight function. CSF's Jeanette Kwek put it this way: An 'ability to anticipate change, to see into the future and be strategically agile is a critical capability for Singapore and the Singapore public service'.[20] The CSF and its predecessor agencies have sought to find clear on-ramps for discussing the future with those with whom they are working. The goal is to improve policy making and decision making by introducing foresight tools and processes that strengthen long-term prospects across the government services they work with.

Much like Dubai, Singapore has evolved its practice in response to changing needs. Historically, Singapore's civil service relied more on developing scenarios in a very traditional practice, but over time the foresight teams have been given more leeway to use other tools and processes that better fit project needs. Kwek notes that, 'There isn't a stickiness to the institution or the form of how the work is done.'[21]

Reflecting on her time in government foresight, Kantar Singapore's Cheryl Chung recalls that much of the work is about 'behavioural interventions' and 'getting people out of their offices and out of their own heads and sharing what they already know'. Chung was not the only person we spoke with who noted that a good amount of foresight work can be as much about empathetic analysis of internal culture and belief systems as it is about finding paths to a preferable future. She told us that when scoping new projects she always adds time for 'communication and management' alongside research and development time, with a personal focus on translating concepts into relatable content for each client.[22]

Similarly, Kwek spoke about the need to be deliberate when framing far-horizon or high-risk events to ensure they are heard in a constructive way. In light of this, CSF frames these as 'emerging strategic issues' (ESIs) to address concerns that might be defined as 'early-warning sign' situations – that is, something that needs to be considered but which may take some preparation to discuss. This approach allows acknowledgement of an emerging issue by putting it on the map, so to speak, with discretion to explore further as needed.

Internally, CSF describes its work path as 'Scout, Challenge and Grow'. Scout is looking at emerging trends. Challenge is questioning mental models and processes. Grow is considered to be no less important than either of the others though, as this is where it sets out to equip public officers with the skills to better think about the future. This approach is one way of building a future culture with intention.[23]

Our futurist colleagues in government service in the UK have a quite different mandate, but they have been equally up to the task of embedding futures awareness into the work they do. The UK government takes a long-term view of the scientific, engineering and infrastructural investments it researches, but is more challenged when considering how the world and society may change over that time horizon and influence the success or failure of those long-term investments.

The government departments and agencies we have worked with in the UK tend to be staffed similarly to those in Singapore, that is, highly-educated scientists, engineers and analysts, which imposes a scientific culture of test and verify, test and verify again. Scientific rigour defines the culture because of the nature of the work. Historically, this damps down capacity for imagination and creativity and elevates risk mitigation as a consideration.

Jim Maltby, Principal Scientist at DSTL, points to a heavy historical reliance on Taylorism, or management through extreme measurement, to optimize performance, which cannot be applied to foresight as a practice. He points to a general belief that, '... you'll improve performance, but in a complex world that just doesn't work at all. It works for manufacturing, but it doesn't work for complex, messy human problems.'[24]

In an effort to build connections with and expand creative capacities around government services, there have been targeted efforts to build networks that open up opportunities for more creative ways of exploring futures for government policy, services and infrastructure. Carney and Maltby in particular have invested heavily in providing space and time outside of office-bound activities to help people feel more comfortable speculating about possibility. In more recent years this culture has begun to shift in some departments, with a growing number turning to more creative methods for futures explorations, leveraging tools such as speculative design, science fiction, immersive media, games and other experiential tools[25] (see Chapter 5).

CHAPTER THREE

Language and communication

Language and communication: what we speak, we create

'Language is a virus', wrote electronic music pioneer Laurie Anderson in a song of the same name, released in 1986.[1] Anderson was channelling Beat Generation writer William S Burroughs, shortening an observation in his 1962 novel *The Ticket That Exploded*, that 'language is a virus from outer space'.[2] Without going down the rabbit hole of Burroughs's ideas about technology and communication, it will suffice to say that both were pointing out how, through human language, ideas take on a life of their own, transmitting from person to person, across cultures, carrying with them various conceptual payloads.

Richard Dawkins reframed this with the term 'meme',[3] playing on a parallel with genes from biology, which transmit, fuse and fragment across ecosystems and generations. As we have seen illustrated all too frequently in recent years, memes, ideas and the constantly mutating language and imagery they contain can be extremely powerful, dare we say infectious, carriers for culture. Both politics and the economy have become dominated by meme warfare, a competition of ideas through seeding and mutation.

As a popular concept, the future itself has myriad subcultures, each represented in our wider culture by a loose conglomeration of images, words, aesthetics, moods, measurements and more. These collections of ideas and impressions, facts-to-be and feelings are what the average person reaches for when they are asked to think or talk about the future. Much of it consists of borrowed ideas or frames, which we may or may not personalize to our own circumstances or aspirations, or within which we see ourselves.

These memes about the future – persistent, shared, transmissible – are what Dutch sociologist Fred Polak called 'images of the future'.[4] They may involve a visual idea, expressed or imagined, about what a future might look like, but they also contain some of the conditions of how these futures come to be, a cluster of information that points towards or illustrates the idea. They are like a soup mix or a box of IKEA furniture – just add context, assemble, and voila! – a future is summoned.

As a practice consisting of mental models and their social negotiation, use of language is as central to building out a future culture as it is the central form of transmission of the lenses, tools, ideas and stories that possible, plausible, probable and preferable futures are made up of. In their book *The Invention of Tomorrow*, Thomas Suddendorf, Jonathan Redshaw and Adam Bulley describe two ways language helps us in futuring. The first is enabling what they call 'nested scenario building', or the ability to imagine alternative future situations and place them inside other futures. The second is through the 'urge to connect',[5] or the desire to share futures we imagine with others. Because of this, language and communication form a crucial part of how people's perceptions of the future get made and remade, and how they become part of the fabric of a social culture.

Words and phrases are often the carriers or labels that represent or illustrate our mental models. They can also represent the tip of the spear of emerging futures. Looking back from early 2023 at the previous few years, we see a global landscape absolutely full of newly coined or newly relevant terms that would have been unintelligible a decade or less prior, generated by everything from rapidly emerging subcultures, the Web3 and crypto booms, to the pandemic, new forms of media and technology, to the war in Ukraine.

Between September 2019 and September 2022, Merriam-Webster Dictionary added over 2,400 new words and phrases.[6] The *Oxford English Dictionary* pulled in slightly more new words, adding over 2,550 to its list over roughly the same period.[7] And that's just in English, which, while among the more elastic languages globally, is only one of approximately 7,000 worldwide. In that short time terms like hopepunk, proof-of-work, sportswashing and ghost kitchen have gone from fringe to common usage on the front pages of newspapers. All of these examples represent trends between two or more sectors coming together to create something new – a phenomenon that is now a more-than-daily occurrence.

> *Words and phrases are often the carriers that represent our mental models.*

GLOSSARY

Ghost kitchen *n.* A business model popular among app-based delivery services where food for multiple restaurants is prepared in a single kitchen not accessible to the public, as a means of optimizing logistics for the delivery services.[8]

Hopepunk *n.* A term coined by Alexandra Rowland in 2017 to describe a genre of speculative literature and art that displays optimism in the face of difficult conditions, as a form of social and political resistance.[9]

Proof-of-work *n.* 'A consensus mechanism used to confirm that network participants, called miners, calculate valid alphanumeric codes – called hashes – to verify bitcoin transactions and add the next block to the blockchain.'[10] The broad concept can be traced to the original bitcoin whitepaper written by Satoshi Nakamoto in 2008, but springs from earlier cryptographic concepts.

Sportswashing *v.* The accusation that particular groups or governments are using sports to gloss over alleged ethical issues, such as crime or human rights abuses.[11]

Becoming familiar with new terms, concepts and ideas can help people negotiate and shift these mental models in useful ways. Being aware of this, and using language to both bring disparate understandings into alignment, and to give currency to new ideas and possibilities, is critical to establishing and feeding a future culture. 'You're asking people to dismantle their own mental models of what their image of the future looks like, which is a scary process,' foresight veteran and educator Cheryl Chung of Kantar Singapore told us, underlining the impact such an effort can have. 'The ability to influence strategic conversation and develop a common vocabulary amongst leadership for decision making is not trivial.'[12]

Getting alignment first

As practitioners, one thing we have observed time and time again is that the ideas and concepts that form the basis for a future culture are more often imported than organic. That is to say, they are brought in through various channels such as engagement with external experts, their texts or talks, aggregated through experiences such as commissioned projects and workshops, or migrated in via the knowledge or training of individuals who join the organization.

In the absence of a formal training programme or educational outreach, people often work off their own assumptions and understandings, and methods or approaches they have picked up elsewhere. The future culture in an organization can sometimes start out looking like a magpie's nest, made up of pieces and parts found and brought-in through disparate ideas and concepts – something we have seen first-hand in online workshops or in-house playbooks of large organizations. Continuing to build with this as the default approach leads to less, not more, alignment around words and ideas.

As an example, we have found this dynamic frequently plays a role in the relative popularity of scenarios as a futuring tool. Fundamentally, scenario means 'story', but in futuring terms a scenario is a well-known tool for defining and assessing alternative futures, which first gained popularity in the 1970s and 80s. How the term is deployed in discussions of the future can range from a general label for one particular outcome or another, to a very specific version of a technique or method.

Scenario is the one term most people have had experience with, through business school, or accessing public scenario reports, or having been part of a scenario exercise somewhere else. However, a range of people called to the same meeting or asked to sign off on a proposed research project may have inherited varied understandings of what the term 'scenario' is referring to, which can contribute to misaligned expectations (What scenario approach did you use, and why was it selected? What did people expect it to do? Did it work or fail the objective?).

Similarly, the word 'trend' can mean wildly different things in a group of just a few people, let alone an organization spread across units or countries. Some take it to mean an economic trend line, while others may understand trend as fad, what's hot right now. Some may have picked up variations from past organizations they've worked in, or a book or report they've read, using *macro-trend*, *megatrend*, or *microtrend* interchangeably, which can create confusion around scale, meaning, time and other factors.

Ensuring that important terms like these are used consistently for fundamental futuring activities – starting with the most direct stakeholders or 'users' of futures work, and spreading out to broader communities within an organization – can be critical to building out the foundation of a future culture, first as an act of user education, but gradually developing more intentional 'speakers' of this language.

FROM IMAGES TO IMAGINARIES

When we start to take these clusters for granted, as accepted futures about which there is little doubt, we get what theorists call an 'imaginary'. Futurist Johannes Kleske describes future imaginaries as 'collective expectations of the future that have become so self-evident that they influence social behavior largely unconsciously and without reflection'.[13]

Imaginaries exist within organizations as well as in societies, as part of the stories through which both operate. They are created by the propagation of language and use of communication forms to embed them, through ads in airports, special sections in newspapers, series on Netflix, conference presentations, profiles of business and technology leaders, political movements, the opinions of experts and forecasters, pop culture references, and so on.

A future culture within an organization will inevitably develop its own future imaginaries. Normally an organization will live with these, often unaltered, for long periods of time – when they become what Peter Schwartz called 'official futures'.[14] A good steward of the future culture recognizes these imaginaries, and tends them, paying attention to their relevance and impact, challenging them with new information, updating when useful, and encouraging new ones to emerge.

Using trust in terminology

Careful attention to language can also be beneficial over time, as it can build trust to be leveraged later. If teammates and stakeholders trust that you have rigorous and credible practices that underpin terminology, that trust can extend into other areas and practices if managed well.

This has often been the case with the terms 'futurist' and 'foresight' themselves when introduced into an organization without an established futuring track record of its own, or a futures team with perceived experiences of past failures. It's not uncommon to have people scoff or ask for a 'test prediction' as a way of distancing themselves from these uncertain practices, or inoculate themselves from 'getting it wrong' in an exercise or discussion. It takes time to build credibility underpinning these terms, which can eventually carry over into trust in deeper engagements.

Jeanette Kwek of Singapore's CSF pointed to the example of her own unit, which was able to use trust in scenario planning among clients to open doors, even as her unit had evolved well beyond this practice. The term had become a trusted brand that could be built on. 'One of our mandates was also to go look for more tools and expand the toolkit. What do we call the toolkit at that point?' recalled Kwek. 'It's called scenario planning plus! Yes, we do scenario planning, and we do all of this other stuff, too.'[15]

This helped open doors, even when the revamped unit's operating name was revised to SPO (a carry-over acronym from the previous name, Scenario Planning Office), which was not as well known. 'When you go to agencies, you're this new organization, semi-new organization, nobody understands what it is you do or who your parent [organization] is, or where you come from, but you pull out the slide that says "scenario planning plus," [and people say] "I know what you mean. You're not that alien. Let me listen to you." There's enough of an anchor of familiarity.'[16]

Choosing your words carefully

Conversely, taking care with popular concepts can be important, especially when internal and external audiences alike latch onto an idea. The past few years have seen a parade of future imaginaries get pumped up, only to fizzle out, or at least fail to live up to the hype.

Joanna Lepore of McDonald's relayed a familiar experience of being careful with buzzwords. For her team's work, she aims for more macro level language that doesn't get as entangled in short-term ebbs and flows of popularity. 'I have a hesitation about this because of the metaverse. I feel like the metaverse worked for and against us in futures and innovation,' she told us. 'First, there was a lot of buzz about it and that worked in our favour. Now, with NFTs, the conversation is like anytime you mention the word metaverse. People say "Oh, here we go again".'[17]

Standardizing around particular keywords and memorable terminology can also help a culture propagate throughout various teams and operating units. Having multiple names for the same idea can create confusion and also set up conflict if synonymous labels become too entrenched. Marketing may talk about 'ChatGPT' and mean all AI-assisted consumer applications, while IT can be discussing LLMs (large language models) at the same time. These are reasonably synonymous concepts from a layperson's point of view, but can take teams down very different paths of conversation, and in the age of intranets and internal sharing platforms, have a very real chance of ending up with overlapping (or hard-to-find) research or analysis floating around internal systems.

We have encountered this regularly in our own work, and take care to consult with clients up front about the dominant language inside their teams or business. In many cases, it's more important to work with the internal culture and harness existing recognition than it is to force fit language.

In a project we describe in Chapter 4, in which we helped design and populate a future signals system for the United Nations Development Program (UNDP), knowing there are already agreed terms and keywords inside the organization helped us tremendously in the early stages. With (ambitiously) thousands of employees and possibly even external partners contributing signals and insights into a system on a weekly basis, maintaining a standard vocabulary helps keep conversations about particular signals and trends and their impacts legible, accessible and unimpeded by confusion or duplication, in much the same way a glossary might. After all, the point of such systems is to enable these conversations, not further entrench difference.

DEALING WITH NEEDLESS BINARIES

At a futures conference in 2022 a famous author was asked by an attendee why most science fiction stories are about dystopias. Her reply was simple: 'Stories need conflict, utopias don't have much conflict.' But is that really true? There are actually quite a lot of sci-fi stories about utopias that have conflict – Ursula K LeGuin's *The Dispossessed* comes to mind – usually because someone is questioning the utopian ideals being imposed, without consideration that other people may have different ideas about what a utopia might be.

We could ask that question about futures work as well. Is it even possible to achieve a utopian future? Imagining *preferable* futures and crafting strategic ways to achieve them actually requires quite a bit of critical assessment. This very much begs the question of 'Who is this preferable future for?' For any given exploration, it's useful to make sure that the 'who' is reasonably defined. It could mean an organization, its stakeholders, customers, or even an entire country.

Scenarios or narratives about the future don't actually need conflict, they need tensions, that is, interesting combinations of trends and their impacts that lead to useful discussions about how the future might play out and where it's best to consider impacts that may alter outcomes, progress or change.

Building scenarios around a perfect world (or an awful one for that matter) are practically useless and provide no valuable insight beyond 'everything is wonderful', with very little sense of how or why it got that way. Scenarios about *interesting* futures are limitless, which is why they are so helpful for examining change over time. Will things go this way, or that way, and what do we do in each case? Even if no scenario is exactly right, considering them critically makes us more agile when a 'real' future happens.

This is not to say that scenarios or narratives must be generally dystopian in nature – far from it – it's just more pragmatic to craft combinatorial scenarios that contain both positive and negative externalities. Since it's impossible to know exactly which future will play out, stretching our muscles to explore scenarios that feature a mixture of progress and stagnation (or backsliding) allows for socialization of possibilities and presents opportunities to examine for whom a particular future might be more positive (or negative). Generally, they are more robust and powerful because they stretch our thinking.

The future is not binary, wholly good or tragically bad, which is why good scenarios also present a mix. Every experience of the future will be unique, so it's helpful to consider multiple perspectives as a way to present richer narratives about what a particular future might feel and look like.

Getting accustomed to the new

Language can also help us get used to the future before it arrives. This can be useful not only when discussing some long-awaited innovation, but in adjusting ourselves to possibly disruptive futures as well. We'll give an example. One of the many difficult, disconcerting elements of the pandemic crisis was one that is often the most overlooked: a lack of preparedness to talk about this difficult future that we suddenly found ourselves in. This doesn't mean talking about pandemics as a possibility, or the need to adapt government or business strategy, but just talking about the new concepts we found ourselves needing to communicate about in order to deal with the myriad aspects of the crisis.

Consider the hundreds of new terms and phrases that we had to wrap our heads around since Covid-19 erupted globally in January 2020, many of which are literally about life and death: *contact tracing*, *superspreader*, *R-number*, *social distancing*, *travel bubbles*, and the list goes on. These weren't just terms thrown about by specialists, they were words all of us, not just doctors and policymakers, needed to understand so we could safely organize ourselves globally, nationally, locally, and within our own homes and families.

Amazingly, hundreds of millions, perhaps billions of people took on these new concepts and phrases in just a few short months. Ignoring their importance, or being slow to internalize them, or having difficulty in conversations about them, could be life-threatening. At the beginning of 2020, these phrases were hardly used outside of medical and scientific practices. By May or June, many were in common usage, and confronting individuals and organizations with hard choices. Many were already known terms, but lacked a global context to bring them to wider usage.

Finding ways to surface and familiarize decision makers in particular, but all members of an organization in general, can help raise their awareness not only of the term or trend in question, but also heighten their awareness of other new signals emerging around them. We talk about this more in Chapter 4, Tools & Knowledge, but using organizational communication tools to encourage the circulation and exchange of emerging terminology can help team members raise their sensitivity to change that is happening around them.

ESTABLISHING CLEAR DEFINITIONS FOR FUZZY CONCEPTS

New words and unfamiliar terms can certainly require some definition, but often it's the words we know and use that can catch us out unless we're careful about the meaning. One of the first points of friction in any collaborative exploration of the future we engage in centres on language and meaning. Assuming we get past a well-scoped definition of 'the future', and sufficiently clear shared understandings of 'signal' and 'trend', our next challenge is usually reckoning with fuzzy terms such as 'horizon', 'impact', 'maturity' and the dreaded 'probability'. For each of these terms, definitions are typically local, meaning they are most meaningfully established within your particular community, organization or ecosystem creating and consuming insights about the future. While it would be nice if we could have universal, standard definitions of these concepts, what you need to understand about a possible future is generally situated around, and defined by the needs of, your organization or community.

Some organizations set these definitions for key metrics clearly, and maintain a commonly agreed measure. For example, the US intelligence community, starting with the CIA, established what they call 'Words on Estimative Probability'[18] in 1964, according to *The Economist*,[19] though the document wasn't shared publicly until 1993. The author of this document, Yale historian and intelligence pioneer Sherman Kent, noted the following about the problems of what he called 'estimative uncertainty': 'It should not come as a surprise that the fact is far from the ideal, that considerable difficulty attends both the fitting of a phrase to the estimators' meaning and the extracting of that meaning by the consumer. Indeed, from the vantage point of almost fourteen years of experience, the difficulties seem practically insurmountable.'[20] As a result of Kent's work, the CIA coalesced around a scale running from 'Certain' to 'Impossible', with five grades of probability in between.

These ratings have been reassessed from time to time by various intelligence offspring and adapted by sister agencies in other countries. In 2005, the Intergovernmental Panel on Climate

Change (IPCC) established its own guidance on expert judgement and uncertainties – incredibly important work as it is how we now understand the IPCC's critical periodic analysis of climate change and its potential impacts.[21] It's worth noting that these organizations prefer words to numbers when talking about probability, as the former provides more flexibility in application, while the latter often get confused with other measures.

This historical analysis looks mostly at issues of probability and validity, but the challenge exists with many kinds of qualitative assessment. Looking back at *How to Future*, we used the term 'impact' 129 times, in probably a dozen contexts, with variable meanings. In only a few of these were we writing specifically about the impact of a trend. How might we define this measure, for example? Impact on whom, measured by what? For one organization, the most important framing of impact might be on customers, users or constituents (e.g. "How significantly might this trend change the behaviour or needs of our users?'), while another might look at impacts on its sector, employees or supply networks. If the word is isolated on its own in a PowerPoint slide or database, alongside an undefined rating, the value of this metric is not only diminished, it can also become a point of confusion ('I'm thinking market impact, while she's thinking internal impact, and neither of us has defined it aloud.').

Clarity and agreement become even more crucial when you involve wider groups or networks of contributors or stakeholders to rate issues by metrics such as 'impact' or 'maturity'. Establishing a general definition and agreed-upon scale, circulating it – and importantly, checking in on it – is important as the analysis of a wider network gets applied to new insights about the future. Does the colleague using a forecast in a planning meeting in San Francisco have the same understanding as that of the forecast's creator in Sydney? Do they have anything to reference as a basic definition or scale, or is everyone going on the hope that they share the same understanding?

Using the examples we explore in greater detail in Chapter 4, we've developed future intelligence platforms meant to be both contributed to and consumed by hundreds or possibly thousands of users. As inputs, outputs and audiences scale, these definitions and metrics need to scale with them, and part of this is clear consultation and communication in establishing and applying them. Never mind examples like San Francisco and Sydney; the same disconnect can occur between parts of the same country or between departments. In a futures context, it often falls to the futures team to define and apply such rating systems, and ensure that the language, metrics and measures used are clear enough – and flexible enough – for widespread application.

Leveraging communication formats

As we lay out above, language is a critical building block of a future culture, as it sends new ideas, terms and even unfamiliar types of communication around the organization. This can be a regular part of the mind-shift needed to push the culture into a more forward-thinking stance. This often takes place through things like trend presentations or scenario reports, the typical artefacts of legacy future culture in business and government.

language is a critical building block of a future culture

These well-recognized communication formats have a particular staying power and currency precisely because they are so familiar. As the most highly-filtered, carefully constructed form of futures media, they are deemed safe to circulate to non-expert hands, and become one of the important early carriers of an internal future culture, inviting a wider audience to align understanding and converge around their meaning.

These mundane tools provide a useful opportunity to create 'affordances' for the future, as we often describe them, borrowing a term from interaction design. This means these formats, when well designed, can constructively introduce new ideas and memorable phrases as a way for non-experts to access or 'carry' a particular idea, insight about or image of the future with them. Often, the names of trends or scenarios will carry on having a life of their own long after the original report or deck is itself out of circulation. They become part of the important internal futures folklore of an organization.

Scenarios can also support memorable labels with concise, rich packages of ideas. Joanna Lepore of McDonald's explained her own approach, which focuses on calibrating language with direct relevance for the business, '... aligning the language, aligning the examples, giving them the "So What?" Giving them a provocation, connecting it into our business, which is the role of the foresight person,' she explained. In this way provocation can be dialled up or down for the audience.[22]

'It goes back to storytelling, how you present foresight,' she told us. 'Foresight is about disrupting people and provoking a different way of thinking. You have to take them outside what they're used to seeing, and get them to emotionally react to something', to land the importance of the insights. She knows something has been well communicated when people ask for a deeper dive. 'They then come to me and say "Oh, hey, I want to know more about that." Or "Do you have any more information on [a new technology], how that's being used or where that's going?" That's the real measure of success for me.'[23]

FLAT-PACK FUTURES

To demonstrate the power of received images, when working with a group new to the methods and mindsets of futuring, and before teaching any concepts or terminology, we occasionally put the ball in the student's court, so to speak, and ask them to describe a day in their future at a particular date to come – say, 2030 or 2050 – and ask them to break it down by parts of the day. What will you be doing on an average morning in 2030, or at midday? What will your work or socializing look like? How will you wrap up the day? Will you commute? Will you be learning or making something? After a few minutes of quiet imagining, people share their own visions of the future.

Spoiler: Rarely are these completely novel visions, but instead represent personalized fusions of widely circulated images. The language is also widely shared and understood within this section of society – AI, hyperloop, algorithm, EV, digital twin, carbon capture, and so on.

These visions are constructed mostly from the building blocks of commonly understood futures, as these are the closest ideas to hand that might be shareable. When asked at short notice to think about the future, unless you are someone who extensively forecasts or engages in creative world-building for a living, you are likely to construct an 'image' using ideas, destinations, language and concepts that have been propagated throughout society by everyone from pop futurists, to advertising creatives, to film directors, to industrial designers, to, well, ambitious billionaires. The power of language and communication in creating persistent and resilient ideas about the future – to transmit 'the virus' – is strong.

This activity isn't meant to catch our students out. Quite the contrary. It's meant to illustrate the power that these images have in our culture, and the value of having your own capacity for futuring in order to develop your own point of view, rather than reflexively building on the views of others. It's also a fun way to start socializing assumptions, generate conversations and open up friendly debates about what's possible and preferable in a given group. It can also be a great way to benchmark a group's progress towards owning their own process for futuring over time.

Driving conversations

In the end, the main value of stimulating the use of future-facing language inside an organization is to drive conversations – to put that language in motion. These conversations are both the day-to-day discussions between colleagues in a hallway, on a call, or on chat, but also the strategic conversations among organizational leadership ('What do we know about X? What threat does Y pose to us long term? Are we going to be the type of company that does Z?').

Building common understanding around the future – and the language needed to describe it – is a fundamental building block of these strategic conversations, according to Mick Costigan of Salesforce. 'There are three parts to any successful strategic conversation,' he told us. 'First, you build shared understanding. [Next] you frame choices, and then make decisions. You can't do more than one at any one time. You have to do them in that sequence. And if you haven't done step one, you won't be able to do step two, it'll fall apart.'[24]

practising 'futuring language' is something that can be done regularly

Future language can't run on an oral culture alone, however. That would just expose the organization to a game of telephone, as different understandings creeping in. Having common resources to consult and places to aggregate what we know about a concept or trend, provides an important common touchpoint to make sure language and knowledge get captured and sufficiently codified so that it forms a common vocabulary. The next chapter will discuss how collections of knowledge, and the platforms they live on, can be a vital 'public square' for future culture.

CULTURE CATALYST: BUILDING A NEW LEXICON

Just as with learning a new language, practising 'futuring language' is something that can be done regularly, in simple ways, to build habits of mind and activate people's awareness of new terms and ideas. Below are two fairly simple activities that can be done as a team or group as culture-building exercises.

Each is intended to invite people who may be non-experts but who are future-curious into conversations about the future. Activities like these with low barriers to entry can have a bigger payoff down the road, inviting people to contribute to building the organization's knowledge and understanding along the way. They can also be soft ways of identifying contributors who manifest some of the qualities we describe in Chapter 2.

• **Word-a-week:** To get people looking and thinking about future signals emerging around them, ask everyone to find one new word or phrase about the future each week, that represents something interesting or previously unknown to them. Set a day to share them, define them and perhaps provide the example they come from. These words or phrases can come from any segment of life – pop culture, new technologies, a new business model or term, politics, and so on. They don't have to pertain directly to the business or focus of the organization, but may indicate a shift that could have significance down the road.

    This discussion can generate interesting conversations about what's going on in the world, where interesting future indicators are emerging, and what different people perceive the importance of these terms and attached signals to be. This can be especially powerful with geographically or culturally dispersed teams, as different concepts and terms can surface in disparate parts of the world at different times. Teams can collect the terms and examples in a place accessible to wider audiences, and even upvote their favourite term each week, or publish a regular glossary. These terms may also point to useful signals for the core futures team to collect in more detail.

• **Neologism sprint:** This exercise goes a step further than the word-a-week, and asks people to either imagine and describe specific scenarios for alternative futures, or choose a year in the future, and place or sector, and imagine the new terms that might emerge (the activity leader could provide these as a prompt to get the ball rolling). Participants define these terms with examples, such as using them in a sentence. These could be just general pop-cultural terms, technical expressions, terms of art or something more specific. They could be job titles or informal roles people might play in a particular future, new product or service categories, idioms or expressions or slang. These can be humorous or serious. They can come from the point of view of a professional, or a particular slice of society – a teenager, gamer or someone new to your society.

As with the word-a-week exercise above, these can be collected, shared, defined and discussed. This may even make a useful icebreaker at an event, workshop or meeting where people are being invited to consider possible futures. The point is to get people thinking creatively about what might emerge in the world around them. In the process of imagining the terms or phrases, participants are actually doing some complex world-building in their minds, but in a way that is low-stress and meant to be fun.

CASE STUDY BBC

Just over 100 years ago, in October 1922, the British Broadcasting Company (now the BBC) 'was formed by a group of leading wireless manufacturers... to produce national radio programming'.[25] From its very inception, the BBC has been an innovative and experimental organization, with an eye towards leveraging new technologies in broadcast media. Today, the BBC has over 22,000 employees with broadcast divisions spanning music, world news, education and original entertainment programming, online media and experimental audio.[26]

The BBC's Research & Development (BBC R&D) department 'is comprised of just over 200 highly specialist research engineers, scientists, ethnographers, designers, producers and innovation professionals working on every aspect of the broadcast chain, from Audiences, Production and Distribution right through to the Programmes themselves'.[27]

Many of those who work at BBC R&D are also heavily invested in creating a future culture throughout the wider organization, so that their work can be more effectively directed towards trajectories for long-term improvement in both engineering and audience innovation. At the tip of the spear for this initiative are two long-time R&D senior producers and creative technologists, Henry Cooke and Libby Miller.

Cooke told us that their group's motivation is to help people at BBC start thinking more productively about the future, noting that R&D is very much about developing new technologies, 'not just transmitters any more'. Their work is increasingly about 'user-facing work and making user-facing prototypes, trying to figure out things about people's future needs'.[28]

Miller added that one of the issues they run into is that their work is perceived as being 'boring', so it's very important to make things more fun by building prototypes and design fiction artefacts that provide opportunities for engagement with new ideas and concepts that look beyond the expected, as well as considering how users might adopt or adapt to change.[29]

Both Miller and Cooke noted that they intentionally push their ideas to be 'as weird as possible' when working on a new project, knowing that once a concept is in the pipeline, a lot of the things that make it interesting are going to get polished down or shaved off. By stretching and pushing in the beginning, there's a better chance that some of the interesting innovations may survive the production process.[30]

Learning the language

Part of their initiative is to tap into the 'collective imagination' of the organization, so they work at tailoring and customizing their language to speak to the particular needs of the group or groups they're working with. Since both Miller and Cooke are technologists by training, they have a better understanding of what types of interaction can help prompt creativity and inventiveness by using exercises that are adapted for those who may find a futuring exercise 'a bit frivolous'. The goal is to use the language of a team to make talking about futures more satisfactory.[31]

Internally, they will sometimes use artefacts or narratives that are quite unexpected and speculative, but for other audiences they will use more mundane objects, to help prompt conversation about what else might change in a future in which this mundane object exists.

Cooke told us that he finds it very rewarding to work with groups that are at first resistant to participating in futures exercises. When someone gets it, 'you know that they're going to become an advocate for these kinds of processes in the future. It's almost more rewarding to crack one person in a fairly resistant group than it is to take it to a group that's on board with you in the first place.'[32]

Taking workshops and exercises out to groups that may initially be resistant is about building trust, learning how to adapt to the vernacular of those groups, and providing proof of value in the process. Over time, this becomes a more organic process. Cooke related that they have built a reputation internally for helping teams expand their mindsets, and that word of mouth has encouraged other teams and divisions to seek them out for learning new creativity techniques and tools, as well as pushing their thinking beyond the 'now'.

Miller stressed that bringing a sense of fun into their work is vital and a really important part of creativity, so they always take time to build workshops and exercises that incorporate activities that provide opportunities to be creative, with freedom to imagine things that might not yield a perfect result, or even be possible, using current technologies. They want people to feel free to try out new things with few constraints.

Diversifying the universe

Cooke and Miller both stressed a priority for bringing in a diversity of voices to their conversations about the future of the BBC. Cooke relayed that 'different teams will have different styles of thinking and different things they think are important or worthwhile. And if you're trying to do this sort of work inside an organization, and you're trying to do capacity building for everybody then you need to have sensitivity to those local conditions.'[33]

Miller added that, 'in order to envision a wider range of possible futures, you need to have as wide and diverse a group of people as you can get into sessions as possible'. Different levels of life experience are vital. In the past, futures exercises happened only at an executive level, which leads to their singular view of what the future will be, and is often very different from almost anyone else's view of what the future will be.[34]

She stressed the importance of making sure that everyone, from C-suite to juniors can participate in sessions, and that they are able to speak frankly and respectfully with each other, and the importance of making space for differing points of view. She accepts that employees generally have 'a certain kind of mindset', and so has been focused recently on working with students and young children as a way to 'imagine a wider range of possible futures'.[35]

This focus on younger audiences became a valuable resource for embracing a futures mindset, when BBC R&D were approached to nominate and create the 100th object for the BBC '100 Objects' project from 2022.[36] Other departments had suggested the other 99 objects, which included objects from BBC history, such as the original radio charter, early microphones, and *Doctor Who* scripts. So together with another colleague, Jasmine Cox, Miller went to primary school students to help create their future object.

'We wanted the work we did with the children to give them a sense of what it is to be an inventor, and to help them imagine their world in 20 years' time, thinking about the positive aspects of what people can achieve, how technology might help us, and how they could see themselves being instrumental in making it happen.'[37]

Cooke reiterated that BBC R&D's futures engagements are intended to start conversations about how both BBC employees and audiences feel about the media they create and consume, as well as new technologies, and social habits around media and entertainment. He pointed out that often, when putting prompts, narratives or artefacts in front of people and discussing them, the conversation turns to personal beliefs, expectations or concerns. The object or prompt creates space for people to think about a 'thing', but the actual topics they end up discussing become quite useful and concrete. Going directly at the topic and discussing specific issues such as data privacy or social habits doesn't generate as wide a range of feedback.[38]

This 'mycorrhizal sampler' is a design fiction intended to read and monitor 'the health of the system of fungi that connects plant roots together'.[39] It was designed by BBC Research and Development, working with primary schools across the UK, to explore their visions of the future and what matters to them. This work informed the decision to make something that tapped into the young people's concerns about the environment, as well as their wish for something that connected people, kept people safe, and helped them be stronger, as well as their interest in what technology could do.[40]

DIFFERENT WAYS OF SEEING THE SAME FUTURE

In the summer of 2020 the International Women's Development Agency (IWDA) was looking for a workshop format to convene groups of participants to examine the impacts of Covid on women, particularly in the Global South. Working with a team of six women futurists from around the world (including Susan Cox-Smith from Changeist), a self-facilitating workshop was developed, then run by IWDA 16 times over 18 months. The resulting insights were then packaged in an online 'zine' to present a set of possible futures, exploring what 'feminist movements need to do differently today to bring these futures into reality'.[41]

IWDA's aim was 'to enable feminist movements to think through the ways in which the Covid-19 crisis is changing possible ways forward into the year 2030 and beyond. Through a new workshop methodology combining futures thinking and intersectional feminist analysis, people across feminist movements have been exploring how Covid-19 is impacting trends we are already seeing take hold – and how we can shape them to create more feminist futures.'[42]

During the development phase, at the suggestion of team member Aarathi Krishnan, a UNDP strategic foresight advisor, a set of 12 'Privileging Forces' was included as additional 'lenses' through which to consider the trends and impacts presented in the workshop. The intention was to give participants a way to consider each trend from different perspectives, in addition to those of which they themselves might be representative. For example, how might paternalism affect efforts to establish federally funded universal childcare? Or, how might ableism impact efforts to address housing precarity for at-risk populations?

These particular lenses were useful to the workshop participants because it afforded them an opportunity to consider how each trend might be perceived by a wider range of people, particularly those who might be impacted by a trend, but whose voices might not be present in the room. By including the privileging forces, more stakeholders could be considered and their needs expressed. The addition of these targeted and specific forces, as defined and understood by the community, provided a way to build a more inclusive way of working.

Building a future culture within an organization works very much in the same way that adding the lenses of privileging forces provided opportunities to be more inclusive in the IWDA workshops. Stretching the futuring mindset throughout an organization builds a network of voices and fosters a sense of inclusivity into the community. This is not to say that teams for specific projects can't be somewhat homogeneous – after all, the IWDA project specifically invited women, primarily from the Global South, working in development or foresight, to think about feminist futures.

What's important about applying additional lenses to a project is that it can be highly valuable for more deeply investigating how a trend or scenario may affect different populations – an organization itself, or its employees, customers or stakeholders – to better understand what is preferable for one may be quite negative or detrimental for another. An example of this is the ExxonMobil scenarios on climate change from the 1970s, which accurately predicted a +/– of 2° temperature rise but then chose to deny its own 'shockingly accurate' climate science with the public.[43]

It should be understood that even when a project is well scoped, using different lenses or considering other perspectives can help to suggest preferable futures that are more robust and appropriate for a wider range of future needs. No project team will ever be fully diverse, even when making an effort to bring in team members from other areas, but they can make their work more inclusive by applying new lenses or perspectives to their work, or sharing their thinking with a wider audience for feedback and input.

CHAPTER FOUR

Tools and knowledge

Tools and platforms: socializing knowledge

Much of futuring, and much about future culture, is social – the product of collective and collaborative sense-making, not individual judgement. If this collective practice of finding and assembling the building blocks of knowledge to describe alternative futures is, as Pierre Wack termed it, 're-perceiving',[1] then a thriving future culture runs on continuous social re-perception.

Much of futuring, and much about future culture, is social

This culture is made up not just of people and practices, but captured and shared insights, data and interpretations. It's not either/or, information collected *or* analysis through social sense-making, but the two fused together. This dynamic has been recognized since the early days of knowledge management and operations research; each cross-disciplinary team of researchers has its own culture, made up of 'human motivations, traditions, habits, expectations', as

RAND analysts John L Kennedy and G L Putt wrote in the mid-1950s about the emergence of research organizations.[2]

How a particular organization's people, history, processes and contexts generate unique ideas and insights *is* that organization's future culture, in effect, a culture that David Sarpong, Mairi Maclean and Elizabeth Alexander call 'perpetually idiosyncratic, amorphous and non-linear' in their research on foresight as a kind of 'way finding' tool.[3] In short, this culture is by nature messy.

Knowledge comes in many flavours

Academic futurists will tell you that knowledge about the future is 'contingent', neither true nor false, but dependent on how the world is unfolding and how it was in the past. This knowledge accrues in real time as the world changes and any good foresight worth the name adapts to change and reflects it as a kind of rolling forward view.

Practicality may mean that describing a view of the future means having to take a snapshot and discuss it – turning it into a list of issues in a presentation or report, a set of scenarios, a road map, or whatever best represents the future you're talking about.

In *How to Future*, we describe in detail three big categories of information about the future:

· Driving forces, or the long-term dynamics that shape or compel trends
· Trends, or emerging or ongoing patterns of change over time
· Signals, or items of information or data points that point towards trends[4]

These three concepts are really only packages of information and observations, collected by groups of people, then described based on a particular point of view. They are dynamic collections of what we think we observe, know or believe. Many different kinds of inputs come together to make up the components of future-related knowledge; at its broadest, it includes all the past knowledge, experiences, intuitions, observations, and anything else members of an organization and its supporting communities contain.

If we focus this down to just what is incoming as a result of open sensing, intentional research, or horizon scanning with a future focus, it still covers quite a large spectrum of types, from quantitative studies, research reports, market data, surveys and such, to the qualitative, including interviews, conference proceedings, expert opinions, social media, observational research, and even art and media. You can find a more in-depth look at these categories and what constitutes them in *How to Future*.

Trapped in the (organizational) matrix

Traditionally, gathering and processing this knowledge and making sense of it was spread across research, marketing, strategy, innovation, R&D and/or a futures team, if the latter existed at all. In public or third sector bodies, this might consist of only research and strategy teams. Even with all the collaborative software and applications we have available today, specialized information is often collected by and trapped in various vertical silos, or circulated in tight loops.

A study might get to the stakeholders with an interest in its contents, but isn't frequently circulated more broadly. A situation report might bounce around a sales or development team, but the interesting signals it contains won't make it to people in other roles who might be able to connect them with other knowledge.

Likewise, software often encourages seeing the world in too flat and logical a framework to surface information for the right people, and AI doesn't yet understand the tacit knowledge a group of people might have that changes the frame of what's useful. In both of these areas, dynamic knowledge gets flattened and reduced to data points, and dynamic relationships get reduced to defined roles.

As inefficient as it might seem to technologists, humans and their internal wetware (brains and nervous systems) remain the best tools we have for observing what's interesting, wrapping it in context, and taking it to someone else who can add to that knowledge to create actionable insight. Sensing and horizon scanning are a great starting point for this.

From our experience, the collecting, analysing, defining, sense-making, arrangement, contextualization and communication of this knowledge is the 'fusion' engine that sits at the core of a future culture, what fuels it and keeps it generating new ways of seeing the world, then prompting fresh decision-making when questions or opportunities emerge.

a future culture is a two-part conversation, one part consensus, one part chaos

Like any good culture, a future culture is a two-part conversation, one part consensus, one part chaos – not a computational process of strict inputs and outputs to be controlled. The more people who can be brought together to add to, use or otherwise engage with these activities, the more they can become involved in continuous development of the future culture in the organization, and the more collective perception, attention and imagination can shift towards the future in the present – leaning the organization into a kind of embodied anticipation.

Engines for culture creation

Futuring runs on inputs such as signals, trends and driving forces. Sensing, or horizon scanning as it is formally known, is the practice of collecting such data. It can take many forms, from casual intake to formal activities and processes. Structured scanning helps draw future maps that feed group sense-making to enable interpretation and anticipatory insights. Digital tools increasingly enable distributed sense-making, allowing the collection and analysis of signals, trends and drivers in real time.

Most tools and methods used in futuring are, at some level, a kind of social object. By that, we mean they are intended to get two or more people talking, and making meaning. Collective meaning-making, in turn, can be a powerful foundation for seeding and growing a future culture inside an organization. However, it doesn't take formally convening a scenario workshop or commissioning a tightly scoped horizon-scanning exercise to create a space for meaning-making about the future. In fact, the perception of these tools as *process* tools, rather than canvases for conversation, can sometimes work against developing an ongoing culture, as it tends to reinforce the notion of futuring as an occasional intervention in standard operating culture, rather than seeing it as creating an intentional cultural fabric.

Practices can start small, and grow with a particular team, or be scaled up as the core of a larger futuring infrastructure. We have seen great examples at different sizes and scales, which fit each particular culture. Starting with knowledge and insight, rather than a set of practices, then filling in with content after provides a common starting point around collective sensing and sense-making, which allows a team or organization to begin building its own frame of understanding the future. This can provide assistance in finding the edges of the knowledge map, or what types of signals, data and insights may be useful over time, and lends to a common language, which we discussed in Chapter 3.

Low-complexity tools for coming together

In both *How to Future* and this book, you will probably notice a bias towards the low-complexity approach. While we do describe some more complex, technology-supported practices below, we've operated with two principles in mind for the last 15 years:

1 Futuring is a social activity first and foremost, and tools should act only as scaffolds or necessary prosthetics for these activities wherever possible and not become a replacement for them.
2 You never know when, where and which tools you will have at hand when engaging in futuring activities – alone, or with others – so being able to collaborate simply, with no material barriers to entry, is optimum.

On the first point, we can hear some readers saying 'Yes, but AI can... (so forth, and so on)!' While we are certainly in a new phase where people are starting to come together around machine-learning tools for experimenting with different forms of creativity and information moulding, we're not yet ready to take the people out of the equation because old-fashioned social cognition still beats anything that AI can bring to the game (so far). On the second point, time and time again, we've arrived in otherwise advanced environments to find a lack of accessible electricity, sparsely available Wi-Fi, malfunctioning displays, overly aggressive firewalls, weirdly textured walls, and so on, which keeps us prepared to work with others in practically any conditions.

As we've all experienced since the age of desktop conferencing and collaboration dawned ('Do you see where I am on the online whiteboard? Can you see my slides?'), technology can get in the way of a group coming together to focus on sense-making, rather than enhancing it. And a last point to emphasize here: the tools you use for futuring shouldn't close down access, but open it, whether it's an issue of differential physical ability, neurodivergence, literacy, cultural familiarity, rank, power, or any difference for that matter.

Any culture is a strong culture when it provides access for the most people to participate, in the widest array of situations.

Card tricks

One simple means of bringing people together around a futuring exercise is by using card-based activities. We've described various card-centred approaches in other venues, based on practices we've been experimenting with as far back as the mid-2000s. Cards invite a kind of useful playfulness into futuring.[5]

Using cards as a vehicle for helping groups become familiar with, combine, sort and otherwise sense-make with both minds and hands creates a kind of instant social connectivity that we see with ordinary games, and calls on our common familiarity with a form with which most people have experience. Because of this, cards can level the playing field, and are legible to most of us. They require little technical expertise. Card-based activities can be performed with a few or even just one person, and their portability allows for social connection and movement. Activities with cards can also be player defined, allowing for new activity construction on the fly. Cards are a natural tool for building narratives.[6]

Changeist and other groups and agencies have created numerous topical and generic card-based decks[7] over the last decade and a half, using them as a way to bring large groups of non-expert participants into futuring exercises (Figure 4.1). These activities have included everything from sharing and comparing trends to building scenarios from dealt hands, to generating prototyping prompts, to sophisticated war-gaming,[8] world-building[9] and problem-solving exercises. These kinds of tabletop activities are very useful in breaking through the distance that has crept into work situations in recent years, and as self-facilitating activities, they are much better for supporting generative thinking in impromptu settings.

Seeding 'imagination infrastructure'

One of the best examples we've seen of building a small but scalable practice of sensing and sense-making about the future

FIGURE 4.1   Futuring cards example

Source: Smithery Ltd (2023)

recently emerged within The National Lottery Community Fund, a public body which, as the name implies, provides grants to organizations throughout the UK. Its mission is to strengthen communities.

The National Lottery Community Fund, and many of its grantees, were shaken by the rolling impacts of the pandemic. Under the guidance of Cassie Robinson, then deputy director of innovation, policy and practice at the Fund, it began taking steps to actively strengthen its capability not only to deal with what it called the emerging 'new normal' but to actively imagine desirable futures and build towards them, rather than continue firefighting alone.

Part of this drive was the creation of the Emerging Futures Fund in early 2020 to, as Robinson described it at the time, 'seed a UK-wide infrastructure for community listening, storytelling and imagining'.[10] The aim was to give these ambitious but sometimes very small groups and organizations a way to extend their own creative vision at a challenging moment for themselves and the communities they serve.

Changeist was fortunate to be brought into the early stages of this process, joined by leading-edge practitioners such as Dr Dan Lockton and Dr Stuart Candy, both then at Carnegie Mellon University, strategic designer Bryan Boyer, and Anab Jain, co-founder of design and experiential futures company Superflux, to work with Fund grantees around futuring and resilience practices.

At the same time as the fund was sharing these practices with its external grantees, Robinson and her team began following the same approach internally, building up both a set of practices and ways of convening to establish a future culture within the Fund itself.

Even as we were speaking with external grantees to encourage foundational futuring practices, Robinson's team put in place the pieces to run their own Scanning & Sensing Network. This network, made of 48 Fund colleagues across the country, set up its own process of scanning by having conversations with a handful of community members each week, identifying important signals of change arising on the landscape and doing a collective sense-making exercise on a weekly basis using a futures framework known as Three Horizons. This work was supported by the futures practitioners International Futures Forum, to share and process what the group had learnt.[11]

Laying down some basic practices as an ongoing ritual, Robinson also created a *Futures Digest*, a fortnightly publication in which insights from the Scanning & Sensing sessions could be shared and new signals from the four nations supported by the Fund (England, Scotland, Wales and Northern Ireland) could be solicited. Additionally, she set up a Futures Club, adding a regular vehicle for the collection and sharing of new insights, as well as a space for a community to emerge around this knowledge and practice.[12] Robinson said the Futures Club was a place where videos from the speaker series could be viewed, new approaches and practices discussed, and practice innovations could be generated.[13]

Nothing more complex than a few short briefings, some simple shared slides, spreadsheets and online canvases were required to participate at the outset. Robinson said these activities were open to all 800 employees of the National Lottery Community Fund, of which about 80 signed up to attend Futures Club sessions.[14]

Robinson's team also launched the Emerging Futures Fund, which was designed to 'build capacity in communities to collectively imagine and shape alternative futures', as well as to demonstrate new modes of funding, and how grant funding could be applied to 'the third horizon'.[15] A total of 52 grantees were awarded with £2 million to carry out place-based experiments to this end.[16]

Some of the ideas and practices tested and validated in the context of the Fund have since become the basis of what a broader movement of practitioners and organizations are calling 'imagination infrastructuring', or the creation of 'a long-term investment in growing and maintaining the capacity of communities and institutions to collectively imagine'.[17]

Putting a collection of practices together that reflected what Fund grantees were doing, then reinforcing an overall posture of facing into the future rather than reacting to the moment is what we think of as building a future culture. The Fund's approach wasn't simply to call on an intervention by external consultants, or stage a one-off exercise in visioning, but to thoughtfully set out a collection of complementary practices that stretched across the immediate team. This playbook is now, in early 2023, involving a wider set of groups and organizations in the UK, particularly at the Joseph Rowntree Foundation, where Robinson has since moved, working with communities to extend this culture and practice under the Imagination Infrastructure banner.[18]

Platforms as cultures

Use of communication tools like Slack and Discord have boomed as workforces have become more distributed in recent years, and as social communities migrate away from open social media to dedicated spaces. While the Slack messaging platform was already growing a substantial enterprise presence, the crypto boom pushed Discord in particular from being a platform best known for supporting gaming communities to the tool of choice for organizing around social tokens, supporting decentralized autonomous organizations (DAOs), an emerging organizational structure that uses crypto tokens as membership mechanisms, and user communities for apps. Both have become platforms for organizing futuring communities, and both host examples of broad-based and functionally specialized groups.

Several people are futuring: Slack

Slack (slack.com) has continued to maintain the feel of a work-place technology, but the ability to link together networks of small firms and independent practitioners, or attendees to an event or conference, or educational workshop participants, has enabled a growing spectrum of futuring practitioners to effec-tively hothouse what can best be described as 'micro-cultures', formed around a particular topic, project or collaboration as social object. We often hear peers make passing references to an interesting signal, link or discussion that they encountered on Slack channels dedicated to futuring. The low barrier to creating a future-focused channel on an organizational Slack – basically a few clicks – makes it easy to set up a space for futures-inclined colleagues to gather, contribute, lurk and learn.

As early adopters of Slack, our own team has brought together long-running relationships with collaborators to form a particu-lar online culture, and also maintained persistent connections through Slack's company-to-company channels as collaborative bridges. Over a period of a decade or more, Slack has helped us build a community of like-minded practitioners, share our own sensing with each other, debate ideas, communicate and support each other's activities, and form ad hoc teams as needed. This persistence itself has generated a kind of internal culture or atmosphere defined by the shared values, interests and short-hand communications of those involved, much as an office culture might evolve if we were all physically co-located.

According to Mick Costigan, Salesforce, which owns the messaging platform, has an internal Slack channel called Futures Lab Community with 'around 1,200 futures-curious people, many of whom have gone through at least one lab, where we share futures news, invite others to do so, and invite participation in these labs'.[19]

We should note, for balance, that we have also seen and been part of Teams-based futures channels and spaces in client organizations, which helpfully allows us to join in on developmental conversations as projects evolve. For us, it's often a less organic and smooth experience, however, given Teams' tight integration with internal knowledge management and resulting access challenges. As with any tech tool, your mileage may vary.

Making future memes: Discord

Discord (discord.com) is an equally sprawling community of communities. As of mid-2023, there are reported to be over 19 million Discord servers running worldwide, hosting 4 billion minutes of conversation each day.[20] Though Discord's founders have been courted by major investors, so far the platform still manages to be the home of the 'anti-Slack' vibe, providing a less productivity-obsessed alternative, though plenty gets done there.

As a lower-cost tool than Slack with a genesis in gaming and pop culture, Discord tends to be the platform of choice for more impromptu or niche communities. The ability to connect it to crypto tokens for access, as mentioned above, also makes the app with the tagline 'Imagine a place...' as the go-to for communities with self-defined internal economies. Futures-focused communities have also found their way into Discord, with some blossoming into quite robust networks of their own.

Futures design group Near Future Laboratory (NFL), with core team members in Spain, Switzerland and the US, has built one example of a futures Discord that has become a rich community of knowledge and practice, bringing together the group's highly experienced internal team with a burgeoning global community of like-minded people. As of early 2023, the NFL Discord now has a population just shy of 1,000 members, having only started in 2020 with a small external network of collaborators and friends.

According to Near Future Laboratory partner Julian Bleecker, its Discord sprang from a pandemic activity the group called Office Hours, a once-a-week open Zoom call with people outside the company who shared an interest in the future. 'During the pandemic, I started doing Office Hours as a way to create connection with people because otherwise I was sitting alone in a studio, as many people were at the time', Bleecker told us in a Slack exchange. (Our own Slack at Changeist has periodically had direct connections not only to our own distributed team, but to NFL, Berlin futures firm Third Wave, UK-based Smithery and other allied partners.)

Bleecker continued, 'One of the guys who was coming to Office Hours said, "You should start a Discord." I sent out invites, and people started showing up, and we figured the community out together. I was understanding the perspective on community, and what it could mean. The desire and purpose seemed the opposite of the social formations that are typically associated with doing creative work today.'[21]

One of the outcomes, Bleecker said, is that the interactions that have been possible within the Discord-based community may help redefine the way the company approaches its own practices going forward. 'We're trying to feel our way into other kinds of structures or practices,' he told us. 'Definitely, in my mind, [the Discord community] has stretched the Near Future Laboratory's way of thinking about our future.'[22]

On the RADAR

An even more radical experiment in building Discord-based knowledge communities for futures can be found in RADAR (radardao.xyz), a DAO established in 2022, from a project called Hyper-link, which was started in 2020, to give independent and corporate trend researchers a common place to share and carry out sense-making around signals of change. RADAR characterizes itself as 'a decentralised global collective of 270+ researchers, early adopters and innovators accelerating better futures'.[23]

As a DAO, RADAR has its own access crypto-token, $SIGNALS, and provides ways for its contributing coterie of agency professionals and soloists to potentially derive economic value as well as community culture, out of participating in an internal economy of signal finders. 'Too often, brilliant futures work is closed off in walled gardens, or even worse, collecting dust on clients' shelves... detached from its creators and curators and disconnected from the trajectory of the world and the people in it',[24] RADAR states on its own Notion-based wiki (notion.so), another artefact of a culture built internationally atop a group of collaborative apps.

The RADAR platform currently hosts dozens of topical threads for its members to explore, publishes trend reports developed by the collective, and is working on a plethora of projects using technologies such as blockchain to create networks of verified topical experts, among many others. As with many DAO-like projects, RADAR is frequently shifting shape and mission, but maintains a core cultural ethos that connects members' insights about the future with a common desire for collaboration over competition, and a desire to play 'an active role in manifesting their reality, not just standing by to witness and record'.[25] This puts RADAR in more of a social innovation category than functioning strictly as a foresight group, observing and analysing trends at arm's length.

Meshing tools together

One of the activities that the BBC R&D futuring team introduced to the wider organization in 2020 was a 'signals gathering group' that convenes about once a month (see Chapter 3 for more on this team's futuring work). According to BBC R&D's Henry Cooke, the group is open to anyone in the organization and, as of early 2023, it continues to gain traction and draw new participants.

The signals group meet in an open, online format using collaborative tool Miro (miro.com) as a common workspace. One thing that's become clearer over time is that the activity has surfaced 'little pockets of people' who may have been doing futures work for years, but without much traction. They are relieved to find out that there are others in the organization who value this work, and are excited to join a community of practice. From May 2021 to September 2022, the group published its collected signals online for anyone to access, and also documented its sense-making process for public consumption, which it continues to add to via occasional public posts on the BBC R&D website.[26]

Cooke said signals gathering becomes a useful way for adding information into a 'possible ideas hopper' and is one of the reasons the people who participate regularly keep coming back, because it helps them build a body of knowledge and inspiration that they can connect to their everyday work. The signal collection becomes a place to socialize ideas and do collective sense-making, a 'ritual' that organically generates conversations that can build over time, leading to the emergence of deeper patterns and connections.[27]

Cooke added that while an online space such as Miro works well for collecting and sorting signals, conversations sparked by sense-making activities flow more freely over chat tools like Slack. He and colleague Libby Miller have worked hard to find the right mix of enabling tools and activities that will speed, not slow, collective imagination.

The key takeaway is to find the collection of tools that can act as a support or storehouse for ideas and insights, and also facilitate conversation about those ideas, but not try to force-fit an activity or behaviour into just one platform. This is especially critical where, like the R&D futuring participants, teams are distributed across many different working locations.

Shaping signal platforms

Many futuring teams may want to stick to shared spreadsheets, presentation decks or collaborative whiteboards as a way to collect and share knowledge. They can subscribe to third-party platform services that supply them with outside collections of trends and signals.

There are several platforms on the market, such as Finland-based Futures Platform (futuresplatform.com) or Canada's Quantumrun (quantumrun.com). Others choose to use the act of signal scanning as an opportunity to harness their own organization's eyes, ears and insights, and design their own platform shaped around their structural needs and interests. In the latter case, one-size-fits-all platforms, with a feed of trends created by third parties, may not fully capture the way a particular team or organization sees the world, nor the way they apply the knowledge captured there – the classic buy-or-build decision point.

Changeist has been involved in creating custom platforms for a number of years, both for our own specific project uses or regional needs, and for clients who want their own. These platforms often involve tools for collecting semi-structured information from horizon scanning and sensing activities, plus the trends and signals content that is generated from this information, with options for visualizing or making sense of trends and signals in ways that suit a particular question or context. The more we have gone through this process, the clearer it becomes that each individual organization's futuring culture has unique needs and ways of bringing people together around futures knowledge, sense-making processes, and application in real-world contexts.

Every organization has unique networks and ecosystems it may interact with.

Every organization also has unique networks and ecosystems it may interact with. Often the practices of both the client organization and its network of partners are in a nascent stage when such tools are developed, which means spending as much time assessing the emergent futuring cultural practices across this ecosystem as structuring taxonomies and specifying technology tool sets. After all, organizations, like individuals, have futures mental models they share – or should share – across the entire organization, which means the way an organization talks about the future, the rituals it uses, the insights it acts on, and the forms this knowledge takes, differ from place to place.

A CONTINUOUSLY CHANGING GARDEN

Along with messaging platforms, note-taking apps have become increasingly popular in recent years. This is particularly true for those that allow notes, for research for example, to be tagged, interconnected, and extended into more complex topical maps. Apps such as Roam Research (roamresearch.com), which calls itself a 'A note-taking tool for networked thought', and Obsidian (obsidian.md), a 'powerful and extensible knowledge base', have gained cult followings because they go beyond simple note management to enable the creation and curation of ongoing, connected graphs of knowledge, allowing the user to understand their – or someone else's – map of collected research, ideas and information in a relational form, and visually, not just textually.

Following on from earlier tools such as Apple's HyperCard, and later, hypertext that spawned the Web, apps like Roam and Obsidian enable users to build knowledge bases over time, and extend the notation of their own thinking as more research and inspiration accretes – a kind of personal or professional wiki that can be created for individual projects, or implemented as running libraries. In both cases, publishing these 'maps' as what are called digital gardens produces a kind of running, searchable horizon scan centred more on relationships between topics mapped than a fixed hierarchy of meaning.

How does this relate to futuring and future cultures? Having observed a handful of futures colleagues use these apps to publish digital gardens over time, this approach represents an elevation of the 'in-progress' aspect of future sensing, shifting emphasis from insights to connections and emergence. This means instead of presenting sensing or other futures research as a finished product, researchers can explore changes in framing and connections over time, as can viewers to whom they provide access. Borrowing a phrase from software engineer Andy Matuschak,[28] futurist Johannes Kleske describes the practice of developing a digital garden using such apps as 'thinking with the garage door up'.[29]

Others we have spoken with about their practices point to collaborative research maps as a useful way to see how other people might make connections or, as Henry Cooke of BBC R&D put it to us, 'plot other routes through', elevating the social cognition aspect of good futures research and sense-making.[30]

'A living database of societal change'

One of the first large-scale exercises we undertook to develop on a custom platform, designed for the futuring culture around it, was for Nesta, the UK-based innovation foundation. Nesta is unique in that its work is structured around three main research missions: innovation in early years education, healthy lifestyles, and sustainable energy transitions for people living in the UK. These three missions are supported from a research and foresight perspective by an internal unit called the Discovery Hub.

Beginning in the spring of 2020, Changeist worked with Nesta to develop a platform to collect and interpret incoming signals relevant to the future of the mission areas, shape them into trends that provide some sense of the currents of emerging or ongoing change, and frame the driving forces that underlie all of this change.

Called the Trends Library, the tool and system we jointly developed was centred around a collaborative platform built using no-code Web-based tools, to provide the Discovery Hub and the mission teams with a living sense-making system. As of early 2023, the Trends Library has grown to contain many hundreds of signals fed by its own 'signal scouts', digested into almost 100 trends across the three mission areas. Nesta has also opened up some sections of the Library as a public tool to stimulate and provoke new ideas among its networks of partners.[31]

Having spent some time looking at how the Discovery Hub worked, how it wanted to interact with mission teams, and how all of these teams might work with external partners, we also integrated some of the tools we've described here, such as Slack and Miro, which Nesta already uses in its own communication and sense-making culture. This enables mission teams to get notional signals into the system easily, without disrupting their workflow, and enables project teams to pull digested trend data from the other end in ways that make it easy to pull into collaborative sense-making spaces.

In an introduction to the public release of the system, Louis Stupple-Harris, foresight engagement lead for the Discovery Hub, described the way Nesta harnesses its teams' awareness of change in their sectors to feed the Trends Library: 'Our signal scouts help us in a multitude of different ways. They help us develop a common language and practice around dealing with future signals, trends and drivers that help us join the dots between different insights across different missions or signals.'[32] Through this, Stupple-Harris said, Nesta's teams can get a better sense of how to act *before* a trend compels a response.

CASE STUDY   United Nations Development Program (UNDP)

As the United Nations' main agency for international development, UNDP operates in over 170 countries, and helps these countries with their own solutions to address human development challenges and achieve the Sustainable Development Goals (SDGs), the 17 interconnected objectives for a sustainable, peaceful future, as one operating objective. As is the case with other UN agencies, UNDP has a history of experimenting with and applying strategic foresight across different groups, programmes and objectives going back a number of years, with different teams taking the initiative to apply their own knowledge of futuring practices, or engage with external specialists on specific projects. The need for foresight has been acknowledged in a range of speeches and strategy documents issued from UNDP leadership, particularly as the challenge of successfully realizing the SDGs has been made more complex by increasing volatility and uncertainty.

'Beyond linear thinking'

In September 2021, UNDP issued its latest Strategic Plan 2022–2025,[33] based on an earlier internal Landscape Paper distilling 11 key global trends. These trends were developed from over 1,000 signals and a set of key drivers collected during research and consultation with partners.[34] Part of the message of this plan was the acknowledgement that UNDP needed to become a more adaptive, agile and anticipatory organization, better equipped to identify emerging risks and learn in real time.

Alongside the Strategic Plan, groups such as the Strategy, Policy & Partnership unit of UNDP's Regional Bureau Asia-Pacific (RBAP) began defining more systematic signals collection processes, using combinations of workshops, online platforms and AI-supported decision-making tools to use signals collection as a way of anticipating emerging risks. These initiatives were based on the hypothesis that 'an anticipatory system pushes us beyond linear thinking, which invests in the most likely short-term scenarios, leaving us vulnerable to unanticipated shocks, towards thinking systematically about potential long-term disruptions'.[35]

As the RBAP team was shaping its own signal-scanning initiatives, the Strategy and Futures Team of UNDP's Executive Office commissioned the development of a cross-organizational platform that could become both a common, dynamic signal collection system *and* a convening 'object' for the organization's 20,000-plus professionals, many of whom work at the front lines of development challenges, in signal-rich environments.

'Activating sensory capabilities'

As the team selected to help develop such a platform, Changeist, as a partner to UK-based Smithery (also a collaborator on the Nesta system), set out in mid-2022 to fashion a comprehensive design with the Strategy and Futures Team, taking into account both the massive scope of intelligence it needs to capture and the diversity of contexts in which it could be used. This platform, which is known as the Future Trends and Signals System, or FTSS, began pilot usage in late 2022, with the initial by-product being UNDP's Global Signals Report issued in early 2023. In that report, the FTSS is described as 'helping activate the sensory capabilities in our global network, bringing to life people's everyday observations of signals of change'.[36]

From the outset, the Strategy and Futures Team saw the FTSS not as a stand-alone tool, but as an enabler of anticipation across the organization. 'Across UNDP, we see staff choosing to bring futures and foresight into their thinking and actions',[37] the team wrote in its vision document describing the system. 'A future-receptive culture is already in the making. Now is the opportunity to connect, cohere and amplify these efforts and establish an ecosystem that considers futures proactively and systematically, enabling UNDP to achieve stronger development impact.'[38] The vision document went on to lay out four key needs for the FTSS:

- **Scan** – take the pulse of the development landscape
- **Prepare** – future analysis and scenarios for emerging issues
- **Influence** – feed foresight into decision making
- **Connect** – create a futures network

Making the vertical horizontal, and decentralized

While the first three of these needs could be addressed in part through designing processes and incentives for participation, the fourth element, creating a futures network, meant paying specific attention to the current and potential social and cultural practices inside UNDP around insight and foresight. For a traditionally mission-oriented organization with a programme-driven culture where information flows from the centre outwards, this would mean designing the FTSS in a way that encourages horizontal flows of knowledge and anticipation – enabling colleagues to feed their own observed signals into the FTSS as front-line scouts.

This meant that they should also be able to take advantage of collective sense-making about the future happening across UNDP in real time. The aim of this change would be to stimulate a culture of anticipation, not just through distributed reports and dashboards, but in how staff and leadership are developed, how teams on the ground are advised and in turn advise their partners, in-country.

The process of designing such a system is iterative. Just creating a new database using generally accepted definitions of 'signal', 'trend', and 'driver' and asking people to bend their ways of working towards these definitions, at best delivers yet another system to report to, and at worst turns people away from collaborating.

Understanding this, one of the goals we set for ourselves on the design side was to break what's become known as Conway's Law, a maxim named after computer scientist M E Conway, who observed in a 1968 article for *Datamation* that, 'Any organization that designs a system will produce a design whose structure is a copy of the organization's internal communications structure.'[39] Though the timelines for piloting the FTSS for early proof-of-concept activities meant building a basic prototype early on and training a cohort to contribute to it, to be successful the whole project team needed to better understand the social and work practices that the FTSS could enhance or enable.

One of the first things our team on the design side – John V Willshire of Smithery and Scott Smith of Changeist – embarked on was a series of in-depth stakeholder interviews across the global organization. This gave us a valuable opportunity to take a representative sample of use cases across UNDP, from a leadership perspective as well as from the point of view of teams experimenting with and implementing new approaches on the ground in very different parts of the world. More importantly, we had a chance to survey what prior and current practices around risk, foresight and innovation looked like, and to understand where in UNDP our early champions sit, beyond those at the top of the organization providing support, resources and sponsorship.

We also quickly turned the basic training for sensing and scanning into more of a studio, where members of the Strategy and Futures Team could regularly come together with the first-wave scanners to review signals, talk about challenges and best practices, and work on initial sense-making. This also provided a venue to understand what motivates and inhibits regular scanning for those involved.

For example, concerns about expertise might hold back someone new to the practice, so providing opportunities to practise and get feedback through the studio meet-ups helped increase confidence. Likewise, setting regular schedules for scanning as teams helped some groups build in social accountability that motivated individuals to make scanning a regular practice. Different teams might adapt variations on these and other practices, but having a set of principles around social practice is the difference between adding a new reporting burden and laying the foundations for a durable, organic future culture.

The preliminary research also told us a lot about what the other end of the FTSS structure – where the insights and sense-making are collected for application to real-world needs – should look like. We learnt the extent to which qualitative insights from the FTSS would need to mesh with the quantitative culture of an organization where economic data is centred. We also learnt the extent to which insights about the future, even quantitative ones, are, to borrow a phrase from writer William Gibson, not evenly distributed. Parts of Latin America, Africa and the Caribbean remain data deserts heavily dependent on only superficial assessments and 'global' or 'rest of world' analysis.

Fashioning new narratives

The 'Prepare' and 'Influence' objectives for the FTSS design also required getting a sense of how strategic conversations and decision making happens in the field as well as the centre, and in what moments the FTSS could help fuel 'What If?' thinking. In particular, how could the FTSS enable the shift from risk-centred thinking towards opportunity-centred thinking?

This meant ensuring the signals and trends developed in the FTSS aren't biased towards emerging disruption or potential crises, but also clearly framing the opportunities that might emerge where development can play a role in policy or programme innovation on the ground. How might better foresight enable better anticipatory opportunity identification?

We needed to be thinking in terms of what is called 'context shaping' inside UNDP, which is identifying key trends and higher-level themes – ways of describing the impacts of related trends on UNDP, its partners and the development landscape – and which are relevant for any given country or challenge.

These 'sets' of context shapers may be different in Peru than in Kazakhstan or East Timor, though they may overlap. Having a better sense of which trends and themes are global, regional or sectoral context shapers, and being able to see how colleagues choose those that resonate, starts to give form to rolling narratives of the present and future as they emerge around the world for UNDP.

Pixels to patterns

As of early 2023, the FTSS is beginning its transition from prototype-as-pilot towards its next phase as a custom-built platform and set of practices and processes. Independent elements are being designed for its three main parts. These are Sensing, where signals come in, are validated, refined, and added to the system, Sense-making, where a curatorial team and users connect signals to trends and bundle trends into different thematic clusters, and Application, where users are able to explore the system, monitor topics, visualize new insights, and package these for use in their day-to-day work (Figure 4.2). Each element will be

FIGURE 4.2　FTSS structure

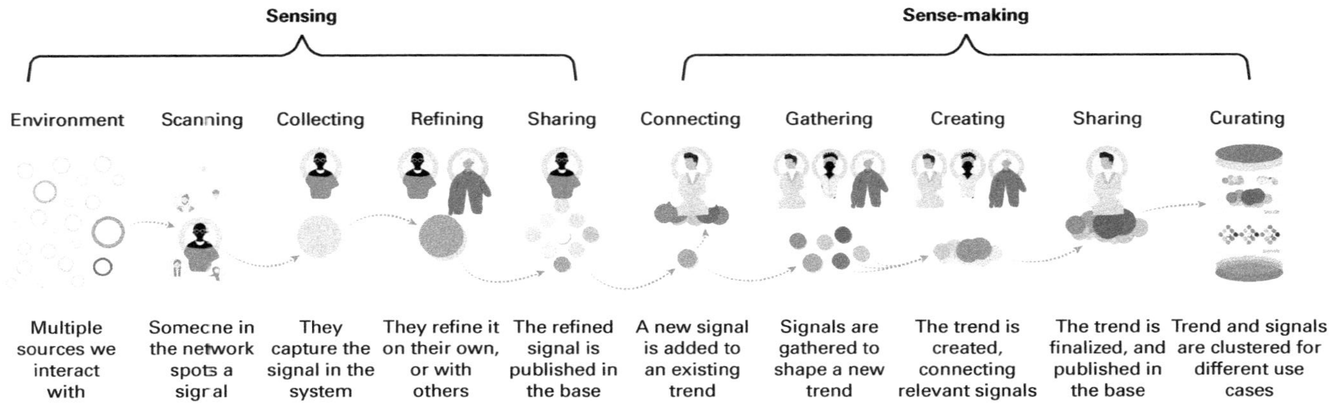

	Sensing				Sense-making			
Environment	Scanning	Collecting	Refining	Sharing	Connecting	Gathering	Creating	Sharing	Curating
Multiple sources we interact with	Someone in the network spots a signal	They capture the signal in the system	They refine it on their own, or with others	The refined signal is published in the base	A new signal is added to an existing trend	Signals are gathered to shape a new trend	The trend is created, connecting relevant signals	The trend is finalized, and published in the base	Trend and signals are clustered for different use cases

Source: Smithery/Changeist (2022)

prototyped and refined over time, and also connected to other UNDP dashboards so that insights and intelligence gathered across different UNDP initiatives globally can flow together in useful ways.

The pilot has already yielded an important early output, called UNDP Signals Spotlight 2023.[40] This work emerged from several months of initial signal collection by a cohort of scanners across UNDP's global staff, followed by a month of intensive sense-making by the Strategy and Futures Team and UNDP Futures Fellows. The Signals Spotlight summarizes 13 emerging strategic themes, touching on everything from the darkening landscape for democracies worldwide, to the impacts of techno-optimism, to regulators venturing into unknown territories, to the emerging tools for climate finance, and beyond. Each of these themes, and the trends and signals underlying them, are framed as dynamic, and subject to change over time.

The selected themes pose important questions about not only the near future of development, but more importantly, what decisions need to be taken in the present in light of their emergence. As the preamble to the report states, 'The point of scanning for signals is not to predict the future. Rather, it is to illuminate a few pixels that stand out in a hazy landscape, pixels that might join up into patterns of plausible futures. Investigating these helps reveal the infinite variety of futures ahead – and where we might be able to steer change in the right direction, towards the future we want.'[41]

The Signals Spotlight is only one of many forms of output the FTSS is designed to generate, with others shaped around different usage moments and purposes, whether developing a country strategy, stress-testing new concepts, briefing country partners, or sparking new innovation concepts. More uses should emerge as early users find new ways to understand and apply the insights they create from it and contribute to it, actively changing the way the organization thinks, works and shapes itself.

CHAPTER FIVE

Space and experience

Spaces and experiences: making places for the future(s)

When was the last time you experienced the past or present through a written factual document, such as a report or presentation? Was this truly embodied, situating you in a 'slice' of a place or experience in a way that stimulated multiple senses, or was it simply a stimulus that drove you to recall other knowledge, or visualize a place or situation in your mind? When was the last time PowerPoint or Zoom provoked an emotional, as well as rational response (not including exasperation at being in yet another meeting, or fear of a family member walking into the shot)? When did you last 'feel' a piece of a possible future in a way that triggered new understanding or insight? Did you share that experience with other people? Was there a collective response?

Today, a small but growing percentage of people are becoming familiar with immersive experiences in a professional setting, as new practices and methodologies spread through the world of foresight, strategy and design. These new practices broadly fall under the heading of 'experiential futures', described by its originators Dr Stuart Candy and Dr Jake Dunagan as a convergence between the needs of futures research and the capabilities afforded by media, design and related tool sets.

This convergence enables us to 'bridge the experiential gulf'[1] between abstraction and feeling. The need for bridging – adding materiality and dimensionality to consideration of futures – emerges because, as Candy and Dunagan put it, futures engagements historically had 'high stakes but low affective engagement and embodied insight. The need for experiential futures is rooted in a challenge inherent to futures work: by definition, it deals with abstractions.'[2]

As the stakes of futuring grow ever higher due to volatility and uncertainty (as discussed in detail in the Introduction), and the volume of information and insights flooding towards any decision maker continues to grow exponentially, the need to break through conceptual barriers and engage people in meaningful debates about *times, things and situations that don't yet exist* becomes ever more valuable. Unlike a focus group with a customer of today, or a test of a product that is already built, the *future* doesn't exist, as futurists like to say. Making meaningful decisions about the future requires other means of engagement, and given that culture is in part made of shared experiences, developing a future culture should extend to include engagement with speculative experiences, spaces and contexts in order to develop collective understandings of the possible.

the future doesn't exist, as futurists like to say.

Making a scene

Before going forward to discuss what role speculative experiences play, it's worth taking a moment to explore something far more concrete: our faulty cognitive tools for prospection. It's true: humans are not very consistent at imagining the long term in any mentally complex way, according to research.[3] But it's actually even a bit more complicated than that, which is why experience becomes an interesting option in the broader future culture toolkit.

First and foremost, modern humans are somewhat well-programmed machines for rapid simulation of the very near future, because we can reference past experiences, according to cognitive scientist Andy Clark. In his 2016 book *Surfing Uncertainty*, Clark describes human decision making as a self-organizing system that utilizes predictive processing, in which the brain is constantly taking in new information about its environment, matching this against experience, and updating its predictive model of what's next.

In doing so, Clark says, the brain is efficient, 'frugal' even, aiming for the minimum viable update to get to the next decision point, as it were.[4] This probably sounds like most organizations you've been in – just trying to use the accumulated data it has to take baby steps, not giant, imaginative leaps. Technically speaking then, we are predictive creatures, just not *that* predictive.

According to researchers, the further out we imagine, the more we struggle to take action, based on what we know may be best for us. Dr Jane McGonigal, director at Institute for the Future (IFTF) and a researcher of cognitive behaviour and futures, high-lights research done to understand why, among other things, we are bad at saving money. According to various brain imaging studies, when we think about our future selves, our brain gradu-ally shuts down the part that thinks about the self in the present, indicating that we start to see our future selves as someone else.[5] How far out in the future this happens – a few years, or a decade – can vary, but the net effect is that we see our future selves as resource competition, which is not exactly conducive to frequent, or empathetic consideration.[6]

We can successfully construct slightly longer timelines, but this happens in bursts – almost as scenes or situations. Just as we can recall certain experiences through what is called 'episodic memory', humans have the capacity to construct scenes of a given future in our minds, through what psychologists Christina Atance and Daniela O'Neill call 'episodic future thinking' (EFT), or 'a projection of the self into the future to pre-experience an event'.[7]

By activating a wide array of the brain's regions, EFT helps us, in the words of Dr McGonigal, to 'pre-feel different possible futures'.[8] In her 2022 book *Imaginable*, McGonigal writes at length about the value of EFT and its benefits to mental health and creativity, positioning it as a capability that can be trained and strengthened through frequent exercise, pushing it to imagine *further* into the future.

Socializing foresight

In Chapter 4 we wrote about the important role that collaborative repositories of knowledge and insight could play in socializing foresight. However, this only represents one dimension. Given the cognitive limitations on prospection described above, social foresight, as futurist Richard Slaughter calls it,[9] can also be built and enriched by shared experiences of possible futures or their component parts – objects, contexts, interactions, sights, sounds, smells, and so on.

These experiences, often spatialized and activating most or all of our senses, reach us individually and collectively on multiple levels. Such experiential futures present us with 'thick' situations (as opposed to the 'thinness' of print or a flat screen alone), with sufficient depth and dimensionality that they can usefully transport us to another time, stretch our imagination, and enhance or extend our perspectives on possibility.

Jake Dunagan, director of the Governance Futures Lab at IFTF, calls these future experiences 'designer cognitive environments',[10] which can be directed (placed in front of you) or ambient (existing around you, perhaps without your initial awareness) interventions that exist within the space between our cognitive capabilities, our culture and the corporeal world.

In a talk at the 2022 Dubai Future Forum, Dunagan laid out a framework for understanding what he calls a 'feedback loop'. This framework includes designing experiential futures to generate authentic, meaningful reactions, creating pathways for learning from those reactions, and staying engaged so that learning can be incorporated into future behaviour.[11] This feedback loop, if applied thoughtfully and at appropriate scale, can be a culture generator of its own, establishing new lenses through which to collectively experience possibility as teams or whole organizational groups.

In the words of Anab Jain, co-founder of design and experiential futures company Superflux, these approaches 'can allow companies and businesses not just to see a flattened idea of a future presented as a graph or a data set, but to experience myriad possibilities. Step into another possible future and really explore it. See it. Feel it. Sense it.'[12] The truly effective element can often be the placing of otherwise scattered trends into context, in relation to each other, in a situation that feels familiar enough – stitching them together into a small piece of another world.

Superflux co-founder Jon Ardern continues, 'You may want to explore the future of X, but the future of X exists within an ecology of other influences and how do they play together.' Jain further emphasizes the power of combining brain and body in the experience. 'Taking people into these futures and giving them a kind of experience or feeling can be emotionally and cognitively different and exciting, and can get you to think and imagine things that you've otherwise not been able to imagine before.'[13]

NAVIGATING TERMINOLOGY

As experiential futures projects proliferate through industry, and more progressive governments and NGOs, terminology in this area has become more muddled. Names of specific applied approaches are sometimes treated as interchangeable, when they actually represent methods which have different aims and intentions.

While a desire to explore more fully, and discover outcomes of value, it's useful to develop a sense of different practices to help decide which may work best for a particular project or team.

Below are four of the most commonly described approaches:

- **Speculative design** – a practice. This is the comparative design of things from futures or alternative pasts or alternative presents for critique.

- **Critical design** – a practice. This is a reflexive use of design to challenge and question social or political assumptions, sometimes, but not always, futures-based.

- **Design fiction** – a tool. Designing fictional things (not purely writing, but material creation such as an object or media), set in a future world, as a means of telling more about that particular future and the forces that shape it.

- **Design futures/futures design** – an approach. Borrowing tools and methods from design to illustrate or materialize future scenarios for exploration.

At Changeist, as non-designers working mostly in non-academic or artistic contexts, we tend to hew towards the term 'design fiction' to describe our own work of creating artefacts drawn from specifically constructed futures for the purposes of exploration and socialization of these futures. The canonical definition of design fiction, given by science fiction author Bruce Sterling, is 'the deliberate use of diegetic prototypes to suspend disbelief about change'. Here, design fiction as a tool borrows from the language of cinema to describe objects that give clues about the world they exist in. This approach, Sterling says, 'tells worlds rather than stories'.[14]

Futures meet strategy

Organizations have been making use of experiential futures approaches for the better part of the past 20 years, though formal language for these tools and practices in a futuring context have only been around since the 2010s. Of course, the idea of prototyping, or modelling an imagined object as a proposition of possible futures goes back to the beginning of human culture, but it was only the emergence of futures as a field, the elevation of design as a democratized practice, and the elision of the two in both innovation and cultural practice that set the table for material exploration of the future in this way.

In our own work, we saw the shift from making prototypes as a way of experiencing and exploring proposed product innovation, such as automotive design and consumer technologies, towards design and futures teams in the mid-2000s working together to materialize objects, media or spaces as a way of better understanding future scenarios or the extrapolation of particular trends. Often, these new practices were a means of enabling teams comprising different disciplines and varying life experiences to interrogate a set of assumptions about, or conditions of, a particular future, from multiple perspectives.

This activity was often directly related to work that was happening down the metaphorical hallway with strategic marketing teams, who were exploring present-day products or media that represented the *future now*, such as innovative food packaging from East Asia, a single-serving product from a bottom-of-the-pyramid market in Africa, or a DIY product hack from a subculture next door. This *innovation scouting* in the present collided with the emerging prototyping practices coming out of the technology industry to spawn ways of generating, as former Google X head of design Nick Foster dubbed them, 'mundane' futures,[15] in order to help people better experience and understand subtle near-future change instead of crashing against sci-fi estrangement.

Public service experiences

A decade or more on, the practice of experiential futures has spread not just into commercial R&D departments and design schools, but government agencies and non-governmental organizations as well. In corporate settings, it has grown as a means of making tangible the collaborations between futures teams and experience designers, formalizing some of the emergent practices of the mid-to-late 2000s.

It also became more widely recognized within higher levels of strategic management as a desirable way of working – taking otherwise abstract scenario work off the page and crafting settings that could be explored more deeply. In the wake of design thinking's heyday as a practice, experiential futures carry some familiar characteristics (working in material forms, often with a human-centred focus), and can function alongside traditional strategy and innovation (see Figure 5.1 for one comparative mapping).

Likewise, designers, futurists and people charged with policy innovation can apply these techniques for the benefit of different publics, not just customers. Governments around the world have been increasing their use of experiential futures as a means of exploring spaces of possibility and prototyping policy for stress-testing (see Chapters 2 and 3 for more on public service futures).

Experiential futures work in commercial settings is often harder to see because many of its uses are in service to advanced design or innovation, and explore areas or topics companies may not be ready to discuss in public. The companies themselves are often intentionally pushing the boundaries of the organization's knowledge or strategy, and can be understandably reluctant to give away commercially sensitive road maps for development. Projects are designed as strategic provocations, in part to spark new thinking or even move or reshape the internal culture of a team or organization.

The humour or uncanniness of an experiential future artefact done well can reframe the way an internal R&D or innovation culture sees possibility, and help that culture 'jump over its own conceptual walls',[16] as Sterling put it in an early essay on these approaches. Often, these jumps are in directions that might otherwise not be sanctioned in traditional strategy discussions,

FIGURE 5.1   A mapping of different techniques and disciplines related to experiential futures and strategy

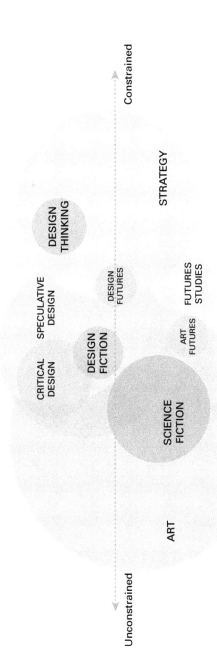

Source: Reproduced with permission of Elliott P Montgomery, 2018

but because of this, they can be quite revealing and useful. Having a shared physical experience of contextualized possibilities can shift mindsets, and potentially the cultural paradigm of an organization itself.

Our own experiences can attest to this, as problems or disagreements that are expressed in familiar formats can dissolve when materialized in an unfamiliar future context. Suspension of disbelief can be a powerful tool. A brand suddenly operating in a new space, a competitor transformed into a future partner, or vice versa, or imagined future needs of a customer expressed in a fictional product can – experienced collectively – change the conversation and shift the culture in subtle ways, now, or down the road.

Suspension of disbelief can be a powerful tool.

While the impact of these practices depends in large part on participants' willingness to use them, the combination of the rational (what we currently know) and intuitive (what we think might be possible) with the emotional (how experiencing these in context make us feel) can be compelling. This is when trust can be vital, which is why it helps to build up to these practices through layering people, ideas, social processes and norms (see Chapter 6). In the words of Superflux's Ardern, describing his own team's client experiences, 'The more trust there is, the more openness there is, and the more courage there is to try new things.'[17]

A FEW WORDS ABOUT CONVERSATIONS

Strategic conversations, including conversations about the future that involve designed experiences, are not like normal conversations. More than just one-sided enthusiasm or dismissal, they are full of delicate tensions, or as futures designer Elliott Montgomery describes them, 'very carefully crafted'[18] and often emotionally freighted. Convening a successful conversation about the future means setting expectations, framing the purpose of the conversation for all parties involved, and often benefits from far more from the convener or leader listening, than by talking.

Such conversations offer an opportunity to step back and consider a future without the fear of directly confronting it in real life, which too often leads to entrenchment and denial rather than open reflection.

Some helpful tips for engaging in these conversations:

- **Conversations aren't votes** – this is something that needs to be expressed in advance, particularly to senior leaders. The futures being put forth are *possible*, but maybe not *probable*. As often happens in scenario workshops, people mistake exploratory narratives for options they need to select from – most people are used to being presented with a list of choices daily. No one is being asked to pick the best or least bad option. Instead, engage with an open mind and learn from the insights that creations represent.

- **Hierarchy takes a back seat** – conversations around futures can be delicate, and involve assumptions and possibilities that often go unspoken. The best conversations will engage voices that are vital, but seldom consulted. This is not an exercise of power. This is a time to hear all sides.

- **Conversation space is a magic circle** – it exists as what the participants and the creators say it is. Hard work is being done to carve out a moment or a few square metres of the future, and hold it for the duration of the experience. The spare meeting room may now be a kitchen of the future, or an exhibition space, or tabletops in a future town hall. Respect this piece of tomorrow and suspend disbelief for as long as it stands.

Making space at different scales

To paraphrase a well-worn meme, one doesn't simply walk into immersive experiential futures. Nor is going 'full immersion' always necessary, practical or desirable. As with other aspects of culture-building we describe in this book, approaches can start small, as appropriate, and build up as confidence and communities grow. Fast and simple has an important time and place alongside the heavily-detailed, careful and considered.

Not everyone will be ready to take a giant leap into artefacts and experiences, but our familiarity with creativity and storytelling developed since birth can be leveraged to build comfort and gradually shift cultural norms around the future, as we've referenced in the examples cited here. If it can work in conservative government departments, banks and NGOs, it can work equally well in other organizations.

IDEAS TO OBJECTS

Often the easiest experiential objects to create are small artefacts that are the output of rapid brainstorming – combining some trends and a time frame to imagine an object, piece of media or short communication that either represents or somehow describes something from the future that emerges. Adding a little detail, perhaps backstory, or widening out the description of the world through discussion or group creativity exercises the necessary mental muscles, and stirs conversation and consideration of challenging topics in ways that engage and stimulate.

We write in greater depth about this in *How to Future*, and provide some canvases there for ideation, but this is a great gateway activity to get people who are unfamiliar with futures work to start mashing ideas together, thinking about the mundane details of how the future emerges in everyday places, and how it is communicated. For straightforward instruction on creating future experiences, we highly recommend Near Future Laboratory's *The Manual of Design Fiction*, which is listed in the Resources section of the book and online.

Everyone thinks about the future in small ways every day, we just don't always realize it.

Many people who might be intimidated by a scenario work-shop can come up with a coherent scenario involving multiple factors or constraints, but will hesitate to credit themselves with the ability. Sometimes, it helps to start by asking a group who they think is going to win a league title next year, or what the price of milk will be in six months. Everyone thinks about the future in small ways every day, we just don't always realize it.

Small things also lend themselves to sharing and display. It's not a difficult task to run a one-hour workshop asking people to generate simple artefacts. This is in fact a way of generating a tremendous amount of discussion, debate, and even interesting potential options for dealing with a challenge or opportunity. This type of engagement also helpfully levels the playing field for experts and newbies alike, thus widening the circle of people involved in your future culture.

OBJECT TO TABLETOP TO EXHIBITION SPACE

Imagine running several workshops on common themes, or having enough people in your workshop or activity to create groups of artefacts along different themes relevant to the same topic. Using a larger set of groups to develop multiple sets of artefacts that 'live' in common settings or situations within a wider world, or that provide different takes on the same future, is a way of engaging more people in world building.

As the details of a particular future world or situation are detailed out, there is space for a wider array of personas and use cases, which opens up more opportunities for interaction with the experience of a range of possible futures, creating something more engaging than a document or talk – something that might actually persist over time, not as a formal business report that people are eager to file away, but an 'event' around which the conversational half-life can be more enduring.

For example, a group of five teams in a healthcare company might explore five different scenarios for the near future of consumer health management, ranging from status quo institution-driven care to completely DIY healthcare mixed and administered by individuals themselves (see Figure 5.2). You can imagine the diversity of health-care products, services or experiences that might exist across this spectrum of possible futures. As each group tackles a scenario, it might develop four or five small artefacts that 'live' in its respective piece of a commonly imagined future, from over-the-counter medica-tion, to new therapies, to packaging, advertising or delivery services.

The end result of this fairly straightforward exercise is the generation of a panoply of imagined future objects that tell a wide-ranging story of the possible futures of this sector. These might range from futures where the organization or brand in question is in full control of its market sector, to one where no need for its current or future capabilities exists.

As a story unfolds, it will speak to possible futures that can be experienced just enough to provoke questions, challenges or further exploration. At a relatively small scale, the rapid creation of physical artefacts and background information on the scenar-ios (key trends, trigger points, impacts) becomes something that more people can engage with, talk about, share, and so on.

Additionally, other people may be invited to visit a space arranged to hold these artefacts and information, providing opportunities for continued conversations and reflection. Imagine how much more engaging this might be than a report or even a presentation deck.

LAYERS OF SOCIAL EXPLORATION

The basic exercise described above has happened in a variety of forms time and time again in organizations practising experien-tial futures over the past decade. Sometimes organizations produce objects to experience, sometimes they develop business plans around more viable ideas, sometimes they create media to share within the organization.

A small selection of artefacts and associated experiences may reveal previously obscured uncertainties by eliciting emotional

FIGURE 5.2   A sketched futures workshop with multiple future explorations

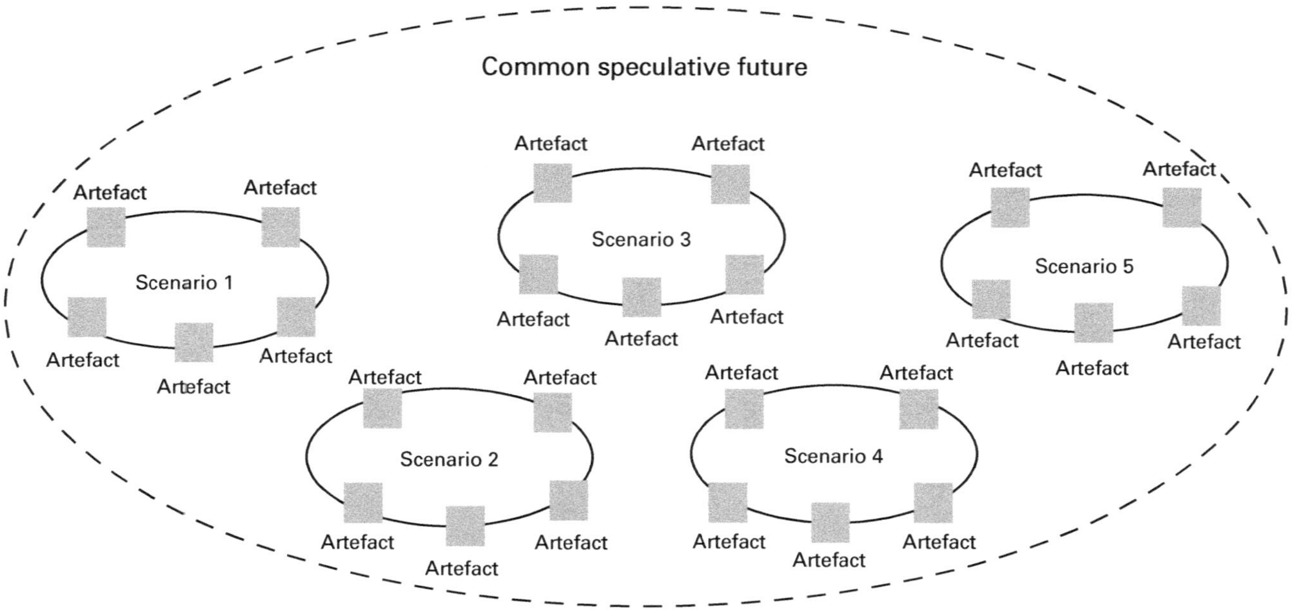

Common speculative future

Scenario 1
Artefact
Artefact
Artefact
Artefact

Scenario 2
Artefact
Artefact
Artefact
Artefact

Scenario 3
Artefact
Artefact
Artefact
Artefact

Scenario 4
Artefact
Artefact
Artefact
Artefact

Scenario 5
Artefact
Artefact
Artefact
Artefact

Source: Changeist (2023)

as well as rational responses. As these small experiences are connected and expanded into a wider collection or narrative, deeper awareness of the opportunities and risks, potential and pitfalls of particular futures emerge. Scaling up demonstrates the complexity of how future situations or worlds may work, inviting further social exploration, and hopefully appreciation of nuances that are less likely to surface when staring at print on screen, or listening to a presentation. Experience encourages exploration.

Among other things, these experiences and exercises in tangibility reveal assumptions, point to blind spots in collective understanding, and strengthen the ability of an organization's future culture to stretch, investigate, provoke and harness collective imagination. Taking examination of the future as something that's done in a distant office or campus building, to something that is co-investigated by many contributors, gives many more people a stake in ideas – and opportunity.

Again, our friend Anab Jain eloquently summarizes both the challenge and chance: 'As temporal myopia thwarts people from imagining what the future might look and feel like, creating opportunities for people to step into an adjacent world combats this inability to conjure long-term visions.'[19]

SPACES FOR REFLECTION

Perhaps the most important reason for using spaces and experiences to explore futures as a way of widening future culture is the opportunity it presents for collective reflection. After all, as much fun as writing stories or making bits of the future can be (or crafting scenarios or collecting trends), the ultimate goals are reflection and, as mentioned in the previous chapter, re-perception.

To imagine holding a thank-you card sent by an elderly villager to a young community volunteer who helped repair her front steps in the wake of a fictional future disaster can trigger a moment of reflection about what relationship we might expect between citizens and an overstretched local government, to use an actual example.[20]

Another case might be encountering a surprising piece of field equipment from an organization you would never expect to encounter in a refugee resettlement camp. One might pause to consider just who could best provide assistance to vulnerable populations in future climate migrations.[21]

Imagine standing with your extended family on the deck of a yet-to-be-built solar energy collection station in Earth orbit, having just arrived via a daily launch from a space facility off the coast of Dubai.[22]

Could these things really happen? What would have to be true? What would need to change, emerge or shift for something like this future situation to be possible? What assumptions that we hold might have to be reconsidered?

As designers Julian Bleecker, Nick Foster, Fabien Girardin and Nicolas Nova explain in their 2023 book *The Manual of Design Fiction*, the value of all of this hard work is surfacing opportunity – it's a chance to put pieces together carefully and thoughtfully, guided by equal parts logic and intuition, and then step back and ask 'So what?' They write: 'There is an opportunity to be more targeted about your objective, more proactive about the conversation you want to have around the completed work.'[23] They go on to suggest having conversations with senior executives if this is happening in a large organization, or a public gathering if this is happening in a municipality or government. These meetings open up opportunities to reflect and discuss – and be sure to capture the discussion if possible. There is gold to be found in this alchemy.

So, as you go about working with spaces and experiences as a layer in your future culture, find the appropriate venue and gathering, and expose others to the experience. Widen the conversation. Expand that culture. We have done all of this and more, and it does have an impact. It is possible to shift and even redefine the norms of using future explorations, which we explore in the next chapter.

EXERCISE   Culture catalyst: Making spaces for futures

There are many different ways you can use space to stimulate collective thinking about the future. We share some here that we've found useful in our practice, or in the spaces occupied by groups we've worked with over the years.

Living maps

In our own work, often with a project or forecast, we build our own space for each exploration when possible. At first, this space is digital, in databases, Google Docs, spreadsheets, Miro boards and the like. Signals jump from online sources into sense-making sticky-note-filled spaces and structures. But inevitably, at some point, the digital becomes physical. Things get converted to paper, stuck on timelines or in thematic clusters, and moved around on walls or tabletops. Those of us who are physically proximate will stand and discuss. Maybe only one or two things move in a week. Sometimes the whole map gets rebuilt to reflect a different understanding. But we use physical space to hold persistent thought. We iterate, go away, think in the shower, street or supermarket and come back to it. Sometimes we'll share online with distant colleagues, pointing the camera at the wall. As long as it's there, the topic remains open for consideration, sometimes for weeks or months.

We recommend this embodied thinking to clients, and practise it with students – building a kind of *war room* to physically represent our thinking to ourselves and others. We build a rough draft road map of a future, and sit with it, taking time when available to question, add and edit. It's our way of cohabitating with a future, where we accept that a given future is contingent, shapeable, subjective. By letting this physical map of the future exist, we acknowledge its contingency and changeability. After all, there are no facts about the future.

Collection spaces

Sometimes what's needed is more than a shared document or database. Creating a physical space that is shared by a team can be a good way to materialize commitment and remind people to share what they think or see. Here are a few examples of using shared space as a place for future speculation to collect and be explored:

- **Signal spaces:** These are simple. Clear a spot on the wall in a common room, clearly label it 'Signal Space' or 'Signals of the Future', or whatever will grab someone's attention, put a few sticky-note pads and pens nearby and give people a task. These can be general things like 'Come in and add a new signal of change you noticed today', or 'Bring examples of the future of [your field or market]'. Make sure everyone is aware of what you mean, and give everyone the responsibility for bringing or suggesting something. With even a small number of people, this space may fill over time. People will stop and read, and maybe comment or build on something. Add photos, data points or other supporting bits. Set a time once a week, maybe Friday lunch or a set coffee break, and have an informal discussion about what's there and what it might mean. Keep track of 'impacts' or implications, and let them collect. Before you know it, you've built a running conversation about the future.

- **Trend walls:** This is the next step. Take a moment to cluster similar signals, and label them with a name. What trend(s) do they point to? What does a particular trend mean for you or your organization? Keep these clusters, reconfigure them, or maybe start to rate them by impact or uncertainty. This embodied sense-making can encourage people to join in and add their own trend suggestions.

- **Provocation walls:** Here, the impacts and implications move to the foreground. This might just be a space where, each week, someone posts one big provocation about the future and everyone has a chance to respond. What if X disappeared in five years? What if people no longer need Y? What if our funding stopped in six months? Again, it's good to explain what you're doing so people don't see hidden messages in your provocations, but making a physical space for alternative futures to live in public can help build comfort or familiarity with possibility and uncertainty.

- **Brand-oriented futures rooms:** This practice dates back some years, and originated with some very present-focused futures clients inside a few big brands. A futures room is often a physical room or space that is commissioned or built temporarily, in which products and other physical items that represent signals about the future relevant to a particular brand's mission or markets are collected and displayed for people throughout the organization to browse. Artefacts of the present can represent something new to a company, or signpost a shift. These rooms take on a life of their own, and can be stimulating to design and populate with items. The very process of setting up a futures room and defining its purpose can help frame group practice by defining what goes in, how it will be presented, to whom, etc. These spaces become places for concentrated futures to assert themselves, to inspire or compel action. Lurking in these spaces means overhearing conversations peppered with phrases like 'I had no idea…' and '… but what if we…'

- **Scenario spaces:** A few years ago we were sitting with some friends in their California lab, showing them some futures cards we'd made for them – a deck of trends, personas and sectors that could be used to build different future scenarios by combining them. We thought they may want to use them in design or futuring sessions. 'We should just put these on a public board for people to play with', our client said. 'Let them make their own little scenarios for fun, maybe they stop on the way to another office and quickly draw a few cards together.' Then, he carried this a step further: 'Hey, maybe we'll just stick one card a week up for people to sketch or leave thoughts and ideas about.' Brilliant. A deck of cards became a public space for play, thought and conversation. Five minutes with each future as you come and go, and the future changes constantly, with every new hand dealt.

- **Object gardens:** This leans on the futures room idea, but is a little more compact and organic. Set aside a tabletop or shelf somewhere public, and give people the task of bringing some object, product or other item that provokes a thought about the future – maybe their kid made it, or they found it in a junk drawer at home. It could be a curious artefact from travel, or a product from a new shop or website. Label the object with a brief descriptor, place it in the object garden, and take a moment each week to share and explain. If you have other people regularly visiting your space, put your object garden in plain view. It might spark a conversation while someone waits for a meeting. You never know.

The point of all of this is to materialize your futuring in ways that give a reminder and make a habit. As you can see, making physical space for the future can help define both cognitive and cultural space. We keep and display images because they hold mental space for memories. We can surely flip this around and find new ways to frame anticipation for the future.

CASE STUDY   Museum of Future Government Services

Perhaps the most advanced, or certainly large-scale, use of experiential futures in policy development has been within the government of Dubai, which began experimenting with the practice around 2010. The first pop-up Museum of Future Government Services was built for the World Government Summit from 2014 to 2017, led by Dr Noah Raford.[24] This ultimately led to investment in a permanent Museum of the Future in 2022 as a way of engaging the public around visions of possible futures.

   Alongside this, the Dubai Future Foundation (DFF), was itself spun out of the Prime Minister's Office, to run a host of programmes designed to advance Dubai's perspective on, and actions for, the future. These include a large-scale public sector accelerator, a media engagement platform, a research think tank, a venture capital fund, a strategy unit and special projects team, plus a training arm named the Dubai Future Academy, which was designed to offer academic programmes to train civil servants and professionals from industry in the UAE to apply futures design to their own innovation work.[25] (NB: Changeist was an initial developer of this curriculum and continues to support regional capacity-building programmes for these cohorts as of 2023.) From these beginnings in 2010 to today, experiential prototypes have travelled from being an experimental idea in the corner of a conference to a way of working that defines Dubai's policy development process and pervades its governance culture.

Dr Raford was a founding executive of the Foundation, its first, then Chief Futurist and Chief Operating Officer. He then went on to hold multiple other roles before retiring from government in 2023. He led the Foundation's futures mission for over a decade and oversaw the growth of many of its strategic projects and institutional programmes, including the Dubai Museum of the Future itself. 'Our entire strategic approach was to translate potential futures into objects, experiences and products that people could experience – right now. That meant something different at the national scale, because these tangible experiences could be assessed for national or city-wide implications and inspire tangible investments and policy change,' he recalled.[26]

'What we realized was that this approach was a far more effective way of getting people's attention and getting them engaged in the issues that we were exploring, because of the nature of the medium. This was particularly powerful if you were modelling or composing something that was aspirational and positive. DFF began using experiential futures as a tool to not only communicate the way the world might change, but to build demand for putting out forward-looking propositions that helped shape policy proposals. We used experiential futures at scale to shift the Overton Window [the current window of acceptable government policies] around what was normally considered possible, and specific design intentions to model what we could do about it now. This turned out to be a tremendously powerful approach, far more than any PowerPoint or consulting report.'[27]

CHAPTER SIX

Rules and norms

Rules and norms: shaping culture

Organizations are in part defined by a set of rules (often constraints or boundaries) and norms (expectations of behaviour). We can think of these as being made up of what's done, what's not done, what's expected, of whom, and how these things are usually carried out.

Organizational culture arises in part from the combination of these things. *Our* way of doing things – actions, rituals and ways of working that are set out in the company handbook, onboarding video, communications around the organization, and so on. Rules and norms may be very strongly expressed, or, as is often the case these days, simply a *vibe*, but they're there to make sure everyone knows what the organization expects, stands for, and will carry on adhering to.

We're not organizational theorists, but in most cases we've experienced across three decades of working in the field, these rules and norms are inherently conservative. This means they are established as a means of keeping things as they are, as agreed by those with power or representation. Rules and norms support and are supported by strategy, and are often stamped on

staying the
same in
the face of
changing
conditions can
be perilous.

structure. The older and more successful the organization is, the higher the probability that these rules and norms are well signposted, and legibly enforced across the culture.

From where we sit, focused on anticipation and adaptation to different emerging forces, this conservative dynamic is in tension with these needs – staying the same in the face of changing conditions can be perilous. Organizational theorists and business historians might respond by saying, 'Well, these businesses succeed because they remain true to their culture as things change around them.' Fair enough. There's definitely something to be said for remaining rooted in convictions.

However, sometimes things have to shift. This top-down conservatism can manifest itself as risk aversion that, in the face of strong headwinds of uncertainty and fundamental change, can be dangerously constricting. Inertia sets in, as does self- and system-protection in the form of risk aversion. Why would a business do anything that risks its hard won positions, individually and collectively? This is very often the case in large, bureaucratic organizations and/or those that have developed around patronage and protection of strong leaders. Inviting risk and uncertainty in the door in the form of adaptation can be perceived as dangerous to the organism and thus be rejected by the system.

As a result, change of important rules and norms lags reality. Equal rights and non-discrimination, equal pay, environmental protection, community responsibility – these are just a few examples where the context changes for many organizations well ahead of the shift in 'the way we do things'. This happens for multiple reasons, whether through conservatism, fear of cost, or simply entrenched comfort with the way things are.

In a less dramatic way, organizations may stick with an 'official future', which futurists define as 'the way things are supposed to be' – this could be the company tagline, the mission statement, or the charter that keeps getting re-chartered – because these rules and norms usually stay in place long past their sell-by date.

Why rules and norms are important for the future

This takes us back to our opening vignette in Chapter 1 about our friend who was aware of returning after our workshop to a culture where his understanding of the roles of risk, uncertainty and the future could clash with those of his team and possibly his leadership. Cultures of systems and organizations don't normally change instantaneously, even if the formal rules change. People take time to learn, digest, and become conscious of their behaviour and the behaviour of others. Effects ripple through, and sometimes don't drive change for a while.

Occasionally, depending on the culture, a 'carrot' can be used, with a change in rules perceived as a way of changing norms. This is a dynamic we've observed in the futures field when futuring skills are included in organizational criteria for promotion and pay increases, but even then, the change is often more mechanical than organic, meaning people may tick a box of adding a new skill, but it doesn't necessarily change their ways of thinking and working. The incentives to apply the new capabilities on an ongoing basis are far fewer than the incentive to be trained in a new skill.

Likewise, recent corporate history is rife with examples of organizations changing the environment, hoping that change in the innovation culture will follow, in effect tinkering with expected norms of social behaviour. Redesigning workspaces to mimic the playful interiors of some Silicon Valley companies is often a 'cargo cult' attempt to recreate spaces where innovation may be happening elsewhere, in hopes of innovation actually springing up in the new location. This mimicking of innovation spaces plays out much like the imitative summoning rituals anthropologists have documented in various cultures over the past century, whereby a symbolic wharf might be built, in hopes that a supply ship would magically arrive.

Here, the expectation is too specific while the change in norms is too diffuse – people won't naturally create breakthrough products and services simply because they have to work in open spaces. Likewise, we've seen that forcing people back to offices post-pandemic doesn't necessarily result in improved productivity.

Establishing a more deep-rooted future culture requires first imagining some desirable norms that might support your future state, thinking about the norms that have taken root in the organization so far, and working on pathways of change (see Culture catalyst below for ways to do this). Comparing these two sets of norms – present and future – can give you a sense of just how much of a journey you may have to embark on. Table 6.1 shows some hypothetical current and future norms for comparison.

TABLE 6.1   Hypothetical current and desired future norms

Current norms	Desired future norms
Focused on maintaining performance history and consistency	Open to variations in performance
Reduction and containment of uncertainty	Seeing uncertainty as a creator of opportunity as well as risk
Limiting unknowns	Probing unknowns
Seeking safety in existing models	Working through experimentation
Demanding exhaustive detail	Comfort with constructive ambiguity
Values disciplinary depth	Values cross-disciplinary expertise

Source: Changeist, 2023

Bottom-up versus top-down change

In the end, changing something as fundamentally *interior* as attitudinal norms requires an effort that is more multifaceted than simply demanding more future-mindedness. There isn't a magic formula, but, as we'll discuss in the Conclusion, it's more of a terrain to cross. In the case studies we've shared in this book, you can see many different routes taken to attempt to propagate new norms of futuring, and attempts to seed future cultures given the allowed starting point and available resources for each type of organization.

There isn't a magic formula, it's more of a terrain to cross.

In our early years of practice, we would work with valiant futures teams (or overworked) individual futurists trying to do their best work, and hoping that the quality and responsiveness to that work would change minds higher up in the organization. Bottom-up efforts could be exhaustive, but with few resources to add to what was already needed to do solid research and create clear, insightful deliverables, little was left at the end of the day for advocating for the value of the work.

And, if we're honest, internal organizational futurists have not always been the best salespeople for their own insights. It's tough to build a movement if you're under-resourced, focused on repeatedly changing objectives and trying to suspend the disbelief of those unfamiliar with *different norms*. The lucky few will have great internal sponsors and message carriers (see the case study below).

Even rarer is strong top-down influence. We've seen the impact this can have in places like Dubai, where the message to civil servants and leaders in the private sector alike can be loud and clear. There, it is literally etched on the exterior of one of the most conspicuous structures in the city, the Museum of the Future. On the surface of the torus-shaped building, Sheik Mohammed, Vice President and Prime Minister of the United

Arab Emirates and ruler of Dubai, enjoins that, 'The future belongs to those who can imagine it, design it and execute it. It isn't something you await, but rather create.'[1]

Even though the operational implications of this message have taken time to cascade through various levels of management and spread out into industry, this conspicuous and oft-repeated call to action reminds every citizen who sees it of the permission they've been given to manifest what they believe that future to be. For Dubai, this mission is a means of thriving and progressing in a challenging neighbourhood in a difficult world.

Having a future culture is a matter of necessity, not one of fashionability.

As described by those we interviewed in Singapore, this hard-wired expectation that the future is a priority also pervades – and gives permission – as to how they should go about their work. And like Dubai, this cultural norm has come about in large part because this dynamic city-state also recognizes its own ongoing risk exposures.

Having a future culture is a matter of necessity, not one of fashionability. As a result, both Dubai and Singapore have developed a strong sense of a common mission internally, and experienced the rewards of being future-focused.

EXERCISE Culture catalyst: prototyping rules and norms

In the previous chapter, we gave an example of prototyping a future brand or business as a way of using a designed experience to move past an obstacle or argument about an organization's future strategy. This worked in part because it created *something* to debate, rather than just a hypothetical argument standing by itself. The same process can be applied by thinking about preferable future rules and norms that will help the culture advance to where it needs to be. Just because they might be abstract doesn't mean they can't be imagined, or described in detail.

In *How to Future*, we offered a canvas called the Scenario Readiness Canvas (also downloadable from howtofuture.com/resources), which became the inspiration for this book's structure. We recommend using it as a way to describe what would be required for a preferable outcome for your brand or organization depending on a particular scenario. It asks useful questions for determining readiness for change. Does the organization have a suitable mix of people and skills, or does useful technology already exist to succeed in a particular future? We included rules in this matrix because they can be critical enabling or inhibiting factors as to whether an organization can succeed in a given future, alongside the right people, tools and networks. One could add norms to this category as well.

A similar exercise can also be useful for imagining shifts in future norms that would be necessary to transition towards a more future-facing organization. This exercise uses a familiar futures tool: backcasting (Figure 6.1). In standard backcasting, you first establish an objective or North Star for the future; for this example we'll choose *Becoming a More Future-Minded Organization.*

In this example we've started at the end and imagined what norm might need to be in place (probably one of many) to enable an organization to be much more future-aware and actively engaged with what's next. For each step, we imagine a necessary enabling norm (which may be a practice, a behaviour or an expectation, for example) that might precede it.

In each case, we're thinking in reverse about enabling: for Y, we would need X to be a norm, and so on, from end to beginning. Your exercise might be completely different, bigger or smaller in scale, focused in other areas, and so on. You might go one step further and think about any rules that might be put in place to secure the norm. The point is to think not just in terms of programmes, tools or staffing, but what this effort may be aiming to establish at a cultural level, helping them to become common practice, and setting expectations for the team or organization as a whole.

FIGURE 6.1 Working backwards to determine necessary norms to become a more future-minded organization

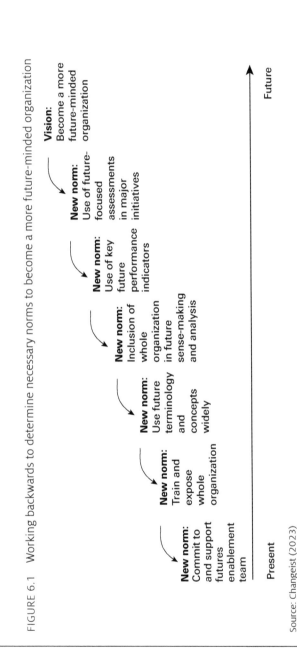

New norm:
Commit to and support futures enablement team

New norm:
Train and expose whole organization

New norm:
Use future terminology and concepts widely

New norm:
Inclusion of whole organization in future sense-making and analysis

New norm:
Use of key future performance indicators

New norm:
Use of future-focused assessments in major initiatives

Vision:
Become a more future-minded organization

Present

Future

Source: Changeist (2023)

THINKING ABOUT FUTURE RULES

Another exercise might be to simply try to imagine any new rules that might be necessary for the organization in a different future. This exercise, while looking at outside requirements, also has implications for internal norms – imagining how an organization or sector might operate in the future means building on the expectations and needs of today, then stretching those in appropriate directions as the particular context suggests.

For example, flying cars will still need speed limits and safety inspections, AI will still need trust and transparency, and suborbital travel will still have to manage crew well-being rules and manage sound regulations. These may only be attenuated to the innovations at hand and expectations of how they should be managed. How might finding your organization under different rules and expectations change the internal norms?

A NORM AS A CHOICE

Imaging new norms, and developing the rules and artefacts that support them, is an intentional act. These things don't just evolve magically, nor are they imposed in most cases. The ground must be prepared, hence our suggestions throughout this book of a series of intentional shifts to help engage people. By encouraging more open and expansive mindsets, conditioning language to help seed different perspectives and comfort levels, opening up communities for future discourse, and providing spaces for future-focused activities and experiences, adoption becomes easier for everyone.

The goal is to gradually change the terrain from one of only present focus to one that leans towards futures. This kind of culture-shifting is gradual, and needs to be considered, both for the necessary drivers and unanticipated impacts. Here is where futures tools can be turned internally, as with the backcasting exercise above, to work out what's needed to make the changes that will drive a preferable future.

CASE STUDY   IBM

IBM has come a long way in just over 100 years. Starting out as a conglomeration of smaller companies making tabulating machines, cash registers and time clocks, Big Blue, as it has long been known, continues to be one of the world's largest providers of information technology (IT) products and services. With over 300,000 employees and expected revenue of $57.4 billion in 2023, IBM remains one of the top five IT services and software providers in the world.[2]

While the company has a long history of applying foresight in focused areas, these efforts tended to surface during times of great societal or technological change, disappearing shortly after, until the next paradigm shift, according to Meghan McGrath, Z Future Demands Lead. In 2020, as the pandemic drove new ways of working, McGrath, along with fellow IBMers Dan Silveira and Roosevelt Faulkner, initiated an effort to bring together a community of colleagues interested in futuring in order to deepen skills in this area and find new ways of applying it.

Rather than set up yet another one-off initiative that might have a short shelf life, the three intentionally looked for ways to work with cultural norms at the company, hoping to align with, rather than conflict with, the company's design thinking culture, which is increasingly embedded in IBM design strategy. The three worked to add new futuring tools and practices to what was already being used, specifically to help grow a future culture that can enhance and complement the company's process and product innovation streams.

McGrath's current role sits within the mainframe business at the strategic level, but she sees herself, along with Silveira and Faulkner, as a catalyst for implementing strategic foresight within the organization as a whole. McGrath joined under the tutelage of Phil Gilbert, who became Head of Design at IBM when his company Lombardi Software was acquired in 2010. He told *Fortune* magazine in 2021, 'What we did [at IBM] was we primarily brought in a new skill set – designers – and we educated the non-designers about the role of designers in the product development process. We integrated designers into the team in a fundamental way… cultural transformation doesn't happen until you put it into practice.'[3]

McGrath sees strategic foresight as a complementary process to design thinking that improves and enhances IBM's products across the board. She told us that IBM as an organization has always tended to embrace a kind of futures thinking in some form. This experience, plus the acculturation to new practices provided by the company's embrace of design thinking as an enabler to business growth provided a pattern language for bringing foresight as both a professional and cultural practice to a broader spectrum of employees. The historical norm of seeking improvement has, as McGrath puts it, 'given us a road map, but I also think it's helped with trust in adoption'.[4]

McGrath recounted that even back in the 1920s when future CEO Thomas J Watson Sr got his start in the industry, he was tasked with thinking of what the future of, or experimental uses for a cash register might be, and what needs its future users might have. This inspired his concept of 'Ever Onward' (which was also memorialized in a song called 'Ever Onward IBM' in 1927).[5]

In 1929, Watson Sr formally created a team called 'Future Demands',[6] which encompassed consideration of all aspects of IBM's business, from possible new technologies that IBM could develop and build, to innovative design and engineering practices, and even to what kind of products IBM itself might create and sell in a future marketplace. He eventually placed responsibility for this team with his son and future CEO, Thomas J Watson Jr[7] during one of the team's most famous episodes: navigating the computer revolution. At a time when the core identity of IBM was tied deeply to calculating machines, it was non-trivial for IBM to move from calculator to computer production. Futures thinking was a part of the process by which the company imagined and then navigated a new identity for its near future self, in order to lead the industry in those early computing years.

One of Faulkner, Silveira and McGrath's first steps in reconnecting with IBM's futures thinking culture was to set up a Strategic Foresight Guild, following the company's long-standing practice of using a 'guild', or community creation model, to bring together disparate groups of people across such a large company who have similar interests – using a template and process already in place.

McGrath noted that when the team began having conversations with executives about creating the Strategic Foresight Guild, they intentionally linked their proposal with the longer history of futures thinking at IBM and referenced the IBM Archives to tap into how this history informed how they wanted to look forward.

McGrath explained her perspective this way: 'I think that a lot of people sense that as we're entering this era of, for example, hybrid cloud, and things are changing in terms of what a data centre looks like and what it means, and what model of business operates there, it actually feels very similar to the calculator and computer debate of the late 1950s.' This broader perspective is 'very identity based… it's a question of: what kind of company can you even imagine that you are?'[8]

By introducing futuring methodologies and tools alongside existing design thinking frameworks, design teams at IBM have built trust with their project teams when developing new initiatives. McGrath told us that participants in workshops or futures thinking activities were often unsure of what to expect, but over time they discovered that there are useful tools and processes that can enrich the work they are already doing.

This sentiment was echoed by her colleagues. 'We found that the design thinking and strategic foresight frameworks can be layered together,' Silveira added. 'You use design thinking as your foundation, and then use strategic foresight to enrich and extend the data past the present and into the future to get new results.'[9]

This experience was valuable and informative for the foresight team, so they worked to help people feel engaged in the process, by making things more playful and allowing buy-in to happen organically, Silveira and Faulkner said. The design teams start with research on their side to help build out a set of impactful shifts in the particular area they might be working in, then, at monthly check-ins, there's time for observations and questions, as well as feedback around what challenges or opportunities could emerge.[10]

According to Faulkner, even the internal messaging around the new Guild and futuring opportunities used similar language and look and feel as other successful internal communications programmes. By signalling that the Guild was a place for learning, and that the community was taking a step-by-step approach to developing skills, Faulkner said the group was able to welcome curious newcomers and build momentum.

This strategy included reinforcing some consistent, simple messages about what the Guild was doing, making sure announcements were regular and clearly branded, and harnessing existing channels for mass distribution across Big Blue's global footprint. Silveira noted that the Guild Slack channel had around 350 participants as of late 2022.[11]

Looking forward, McGrath has observed that more and more often the value of foresight work is in anticipating change more effectively, especially in spaces that are moving swiftly, such as security, financial transactions or quantum computing. It is not uncommon for the market to change significantly in the time between a product or service first being imagined and when it is finally launched. Using futures thinking approaches, engineers in these spaces can become better at anticipating what their challenges may be, six months or even six years down the road. They also find that collaboration across divisions is more constructive for designing product improvements and documenting stakeholder impacts.

McGrath told us that doing foresight work is, 'helping to prioritize where we're going and how, using futures thinking, we can get there. It's a sort of constant progression. Organizations don't reach futuring maturity overnight, but through growing the work and learning as they go along...'[12]

She pointed out that she finds Terry Grim's Foresight Maturity Model[13] to be a perfect tool for their work, as Grim 'was in IBM management and senior positions for a long time and has a very good sense of how something like this would scale up in a company like IBM'. McGrath finds it very useful for measuring both impacts and progress. She also noted that Jerome Glenn's Implications Wheel,[14] (aka Futures Wheel, or Impact Wheel – see *How to Future* for more detail on this tool), backcasting and Sohail Inayatullah's Causal Layered Analysis[15] are effective tools IBM's guild are using more over time.[16]

Silveira and Faulkner explained that in order to build familiarity and ensure colleagues had their own sense of when and where to use them, each of these methods were explored in the Guild.

The Strategic Foresight team also worked with non-product units to apply futuring approaches to other issues. One example Faulkner shared was work they were invited to support with IBM's Racial Equity in Design team around advancing equity policies. Using trends the team brought in, and a Futures Wheel exercise, the racial equity design team worked for two hours to develop eight stories about future racial equity, with one participant illustrating the stories in graphic novel form.

Silveira said the workshop was incredibly useful in surfacing participants' assumptions and visions of what racial equity means to them, helping to bring those assumptions into the collective conversation about this critical issue.

McGrath suggests that with strategic foresight work, it's important that people are given a chance to have an embodied experience in which they can leave thinking about something differently than when they started. This helps grow advocacy for the process.

If a product team wants to work with designers using strategic foresight, they have to be willing to invest time and resources, and acknowledge what they have learnt in the process, because otherwise nothing will come from it. In the end, it won't benefit a team, and it won't build trust in the process itself. As one executive told McGrath: 'You want to plant seeds where they can actually grow.'[17]

McGrath affirmed that there's interest in strategic foresight from the business and marketing teams too, because it supplements how they think about organizational change over time. They know that traditionally, the designers have been the canaries in the coal mine, she said, and incorporating strategic foresight as a practice helps inform the organization and keep it resilient in times of change.

IBM as an organization has managed to steer through big paradigm shifts multiple times in its history, and has successfully transitioned to new businesses and business models as the landscape for technology has changed. Much of this can be attributed to how well the organization navigates through change, even if internally it is happening slowly. The ability to see change coming, to imagine possible and preferable futures, is a key reason to promote and support future culture. Even if thinking about the future has never been an aspect of an organization, there's no better time to start than now.

CHAPTER SEVEN

Networks and ecosystems

Networks and ecosystems: building webs of support

The term 'business ecosystem' seems pervasive today, but it only appeared in the early 1990s, coined by James Moore in his article for *Harvard Business Review*, 'Predators and prey: A new ecology of competition'.[1] Keeping with the Darwinian title of the piece, Moore leaned heavily on metaphors from evolution and biology to describe the systems of support and reliance that emerge around organizations, primarily commercial ones.

Thirty years ago, this was a novel lens, emerging from the heyday of US business schools and analysts studying the powerful business networks of East Asia, and the emergence of similar, though less rigid, support networks that grew up around Silicon Valley. Moore described ecosystems of competition, growth and market dominance. Here, we're discussing something softer edged but critically important: networks and ecosystems of support.

Why softer edged? Well, sadly, no one but the seriously misinformed would characterize the field of futures as a raging money-gusher – though there are plenty of recent critiques of so-called 'corporate futurism'. Rather, it's a capability that very much plays a supporting role to decision making, whether in strategy, policy, innovation or other areas of critical decision making. It's more of a brain than an engine room, and is often called upon in edge cases, as in very early front-end exploration for innovation, or to reduce the scope of *known unknowns*, things the organization recognizes it doesn't understand sufficiently.

It's more of a brain than an engine room

As we've described throughout this book, directly and through the words of those working in this function, much futures work *requires* support, even as it supports others. More often than not, if they grow at all, futures teams hit a point where they need an ecosystem of support if they are to thrive, maybe more than just about any other organizational function.

NETWORK VERSUS ECOSYSTEM

We're using both terms here, but what's the difference?

In this context, we tend to use the word network to refer to a relatively fixed set of relationships that are trusted – like a vetted network of experts or practitioners on whom a person or organization relies for certain capabilities. Networks may unravel if a critical node disappears.

Here, ecosystem stands in for a rich system of varied support resources that enrich each other's capabilities in the context of their cooperation or collaboration. Entities in an ecosystem may come and go, but its strength arises from connections, proximity and/or exchange with other members of the ecosystem. Ecosystems may survive by replacing important participants that disappear or fall out of the ecosystem.

Let's reflect on some of the characteristics of internal futurists and teams we described in Chapter 1. These people or entities are expected to be different by design from the organization they exist within. They should be norm challengers – not a great way to build networks of friends, unless those friends value new ideas greatly. To be norm challengers, they should maintain a fresh stock of new ideas, insights and influences from outside the organizational atmosphere. They should be looking for examples of new approaches, new models, deviant behaviours and other 'alien artefacts'. They will often be more like their peers elsewhere in the field than like their colleagues; maintaining outsider status and connection is important.

Given these expectations and norms, building bridges of support both inside and outside an organization is critical to growth and survival for a futures team or function. This doesn't come through osmosis or random interaction, however much an organization might rely on the energy and creativity of people staffing these teams. Futures leaders inside organizations need trusted relationships, flows of information, skills and points of view far faster than they might be able to cultivate them internally. This is particularly true as exploration too far afield from the organization's internally accepted point of view, or expertise in specialist methodologies, can appear to be a risky investment to develop and maintain in-house.

Inside and outside networks and ecosystems

Two kinds of networks and ecosystems are important in growing and maintaining a strong, thriving future culture. The first kind is external. External networks are built on carefully cultivated relationships with what might be called 'vendors' in procurement-speak, a network constituted of trusted past and current suppliers across the spectrum of needs, from hard research to soft interpretation, from textual and quantitative, to visual and experiential (and doubtless along many more dimensions).

These networks also include subject-matter experts, academics, professionals, social and other scientists, artists, designers, writers, filmmakers, philosophers, policymakers, financial experts and much more. They can provide sets of lenses on problems that can't be found inside the organization, and have experience going deep into places or subjects that organizations can't – they bring the outside in. They tend to be people whose knowledge and ways of seeing the world are valued by the futures leader for what they can bring to the table. They also tend to be people with a realistic view of how organizations work, and can attenuate their insights and expectations to this understanding.

These individuals and small groups tend to exist within the broader external ecosystem that is also necessary. An ecosystem tends to be made up of organizations that enrich the value of the surrounding systems, such as organizations with dynamic research capabilities (institutes, think tanks, universities), and those that generate creative output, such as new art and media that can reframe knowledge and materialize critiques of emerging issues in new ways. They may be next door, or around the world, but relationships within an ecosystem can cross-pollinate and provide a great deal of fresh thinking and dare we say it, inspiration that can keep a strong futures culture fuelled with intellectual nutrients.

Internal networks can take a heavy effort to create and maintain. Throughout our research for this book, we've heard from professionals at the front lines of future cultures, both new and established, about the importance of cultivating a network of supportive stakeholders, ambassadors and like-minded mentors and advocates. These people can carry the value of a team's work to higher and deeper levels of an organization, provide role models for others to look to when judging value, and hold strategic space for the work that needs to be done.

Strategies for finding these people inside the organization may be similar to those of sourcing good team members. Look for people with the qualities we outlined in Chapter 2 – the curious, the people with demonstrated awareness that extends beyond their professional role, the systems thinkers, those with longer mental timelines.

We've heard over and over that the best advocates are the people who have a stake in the future beyond the organization. 'They care a lot about the future, and about influencing the future,' Joanna Lepore told us of her key stakeholders at McDonald's. 'They're really very convinced about the fact that we can make a differ-

the best advocates are people who have a stake in the future beyond the organization.

ence from inside the organization, that we're not just cogs in the machine. And that the future is not linear. That we can make change, we can transform it.'[2]

These internal networks may become the scaffolding for internal ecosystems over time. Individual supporters and sponsors become part of broader groups of interest and support. Internal resource networks open up into ecosystems that understand the value of the future culture, and become important 'tent pegs' helping to keep it in place and give it weight and substance.

This may include, for example, a communications team, R&D arm, market research teams, design, and so on, all of whom may benefit from different pieces of the same explorations at different points, but who through these explorations of the future have a common interest. These key ecosystem nodes may not be within the specific organization itself, but within organizational networks – in places like government entities, agencies or large NGOs.

All of this, of course, puts an extra burden on a futures leader and their team. It's a job of careful networking and network-weaving, of sourcing, listening, reviewing, following threads, and providing support to all parts of the web they create. On the other hand, through this effort, a futures leader can create and extend a system of value and influence that helps root their work in the wider organization, and carry that system with them if and when they move on to another challenge.

EXERCISE   Culture catalyst: Sketching networks and ecosystems

As with recruitment, networks are often hard to plan in advance. Unlike recruitment, a map of a given network or ecosystem may exist largely in the mind of the futures leader or team. This is where it might be valuable to take an hour or have an informal offsite session to get ahead of the game and map out what exists, and what is preferable or possible in the future.

A useful starting point might be to begin by listing a set of desirable characteristics or capabilities internally and externally. These may be similar, but not the same list. The characteristics laid out in Chapter 3 can help you build out your list. Then, note or sketch out your internal network and, if possible, ecosystem. Refer to the box above for clarifying definitions. Then do the same for external networks and ecosystems. This might be on the left and right side of the same whiteboard.

Next, looking at the list of desirable characteristics or capabilities, look at how the nodes on each side match up or rate. Is a piece of the system there because it's what you inherited? What you want? What have you cultivated? How much do both match your aspiration? What can be changed?

any good operation needs to build out its base

Last, maybe sketch out the missing pieces, or even the 'moonshot' relationships. Who would you bring in if you could? What would that require, in terms of connections and resources? How long might completing the desired network take, and who or what can help you get there? Where are the situations where those connections might be made?

Running through an exercise like this can help make visible the aspirations and assumptions of you and your team. After all, any good operation needs to build out its base, and that helps everyone work off the same map!

FUTURES ECOSYSTEMS YESTERDAY, TODAY AND TOMORROW

Futures groups have relied on ecosystems and networks since their emergence in the 1940s. RAND Corporation (the name is a contraction of 'research and development'), often pointed to as one of the original 'futurist' organizations, was created first as a project within, and then as a spin-out of, Douglas Aircraft, an acknowledgement that it was being called upon to support a wider network of policymakers in the aftermath of World War II.[3]

Situated within a booming post-war network of Southern California universities, emerging aerospace and technology enterprises in Los Angeles and up and down the west coast, and with networks across academia, government and industry, early RAND built its capabilities by having access to the intellectual firepower of these networks, recruiting both men and women with strong research backgrounds and somewhat eclectic skills. It was also helped to thrive by the circulation through its halls of its networks' networks, and quickly became a place where various brain trusts assembled in service to the US war effort to find support for their continued research.

Likewise, the Institute for the Future (IFTF), another of the original wave of futures research groups still in operation, was spun out of RAND 20 years later in 1968, with original funding support from Ford Foundation, and a core of three ex-RAND researchers, Paul Baran, Olaf Helmer and Ted Gordon.[4] Similar to RAND, IFTF built deep relationships with government research organizations such as the National Science Foundation and the Advanced Research Projects Agency (ARPA), now called DARPA. Based in Palo Alto, California, in the heart of the technology industry, IFTF has benefitted from a close association with industry, government and academia over its half-century of existence.

Most of today's futures firms are smaller, with many boutique firms and recent start-ups coming out of design or policy environments. Our own experience is that of an ecosystem of networks, with different regional clusters sitting in proximity to government, industry and academia, but also connecting with each other.

We tend to work with small groups of practitioners and independent researchers or creatives, in different combinations, to take advantage of particular subject-matter or professional expertise. On occasion, we collaborate with other agency teams, sometimes at the request of clients themselves who might be particularly familiar with the service provider landscape.

Despite being in economic competition, in segments of the futures field, there is a high degree of collaboration or co-opetition, defined as collaboration among competitors to reach a common goal.[5] Some larger entities, such as government agencies, will intentionally select expertise from different companies or agencies as a way to bring the best talent to bear on a challenging project, not unlike the 1950s or 1960s.

Absent the rise of another major think tank or super-agency, it's likely that the futures field will evolve even further towards ecosystems and networks of collaboration, as both needs and methodologies become more specialized. Challenges are evolving faster than stakeholders' understanding and insight, and faster than the biggest strategy firms can meaningfully adapt. Keeping an ecosystem of diverse practitioners with a range of subject-matter expertise and practices will likely continue to be the smart strategy as organizations look for more choice in their approaches to problem definition and option identification in the coming decade.

CASE STUDY   AXA Foresight

AXA is one of the world's largest insurance and financial services providers, based in Paris, France, with revenues of around €102 billion in 2022, serving 95 million customers worldwide, with business operations in dozens of countries, and almost 120,000 employees.[6] AXA is effectively in the business of risk management. At its global scale, the company is also an active mover not only in financial markets, but increasingly in the social and environmental contexts of many of its customers, what group Head of Foresight for the company, Olivier Desbiey, calls 'a responsible social player as an organization'.[7]

This societal role influences the research agenda that Desbiey, his direct team, and allies within closely related parts of the organization, such as the AXA Research Fund, pursue. The group looks at long-term trends that could impact AXA as an insurer, such as climate risk, but also as an employer and social actor. For Desbiey's team, communication – inside the company, with partners and the outside market – plays an important role in establishing a future culture and sets the agenda for the company's broader ecosystem.

AXA's Foresight group leverages this network of both internal and external contributors to help validate its focus while also framing the terms of discussion, by signalling what topics AXA is prioritizing, and to show how the company is engaging with emerging future themes, as it has done in recent years with topics such as urbanization, mental health and social cohesion.

Desbiey explained that as a small team within a much larger organization, they '... usually join forces with other people and teams in more- or less-structured communities. It is a two-way street, as it allows us to expand the scope of our foresight activities, relying on broader expertise and backgrounds to better disseminate our own work and analysis.'[8]

He outlined for us the five areas on which their Foresight network is comprised and how they work with each other to provide a robust ecosystem for collaboration on future-oriented projects, and communication to wider audiences both internally and externally:

- **AXA Teams with a forward-looking agenda:** This includes the AXA Research Fund, the Group Emerging Risks Team and the Group Threat Anticipation Team. These teams meet on a regular basis, every six weeks or so, to align agendas and identify potential collaboration, but are not a formal committee as such.

- **AXA Foresight Communities:** These communities are based on topics of interest in connection with the foresight studies AXA has conducted and are topically relevant to current work. This included health subject-matter experts when AXA worked on mental health in 2020, IT and tech people for the Metaverse project, and sustainability experts for the Future of ESG. These communities are shorter term and project based and help the group focus on relevant insights and recommendations for AXA in its analysis.

- **AXA Monthly Foresight Newsletter subscribers:** This network includes around 3,000 colleagues worldwide who are interested in knowing more about foresight. The newsletter is more general interest, but also occasionally covers focused topics.

- **External Head of Foresight Network:** This group consists of people from various organizations (e.g. big corporations, public institutions) sharing the same approach to foresight, that is, exploring possible futures by leveraging social sciences on societal issues. This is an informal network, which meets on a quarterly basis to share news and current priorities.

- **External Partners:** These partnerships consist of external consultancies, which have various objectives and are engaged for collaborating or participating in foresight explorations, for learning and building foresight capabilities and strengthening thought leadership in connection with AXA's annual foresight report.

The Foresight team has also built a strong relationship with AXA's communications team, working to frame explorations that can help shape external opinion and ideas. 'We want to highlight the bigger context in which AXA will be evolving in the future,' Desbiey told us. 'It's important to be able to have this voice externally to give an idea of what the AXA vision for the future is.'[9]

As a global company, Desbiey pointed out that sometimes the most effective way to reach far-flung colleagues is through the influence of external thought leadership. 'We successfully meet our objective in terms of external communication, and we generally receive excellent feedback on our publications.'[10] These include a visually engaging report on the nature of progress, released in 2022, called ProgressLand.[11]

'If a colleague hasn't heard about a particular foresight project or research themes through internal channels, seeing it in the outside press, or accessing a public webinar can also bring them into the loop,' Desbiey said. '[The Foresight team] are close to our friends in communication for the brand, and it really helps us to propagate our content, be it for external audiences or for our colleagues.'[12]

Meanwhile, the group is creating resources to educate colleagues around future trends and also build capacity. A partnership with the

Copenhagen Institute for Futures Studies to train AXA team members in futures tools is augmented by a growing digital library of publications and research looking at timely themes.[13] Desbiey said his team is also trying to create content that is more 'snackable', such as short social videos and quick scenario summaries, in an effort to keep future issues top of mind among his colleagues in the daily competition with other feeds of information.[14]

Conclusion
Maintaining momentum

Developing a sustainable and enduring future culture is no easy task, and what we have outlined in this book only scratches the surface. There is no quick workshop, magic call-to-action or bright LinkedIn graphic that will make it happen. All culture-building is work, and in this case, it involves moving not just collective mental models, but how they function together as practice and ritual. We don't write this to put you off, but to clarify that building future cultures is a process that requires clear intention and direction, patience and care.

building future cultures requires clear intention and direction, patience and care.

As we stated at the outset, this is also a challenge of managing tensions, in this case the tension between short-term execution and long-term vision. Optimally, these two should be in alignment, but market cross-winds will push short-term objectives to and fro, and long-term vision can and should adapt to the conditions this work anticipates.

The challenge is to become better organizationally at maintaining what futurist Jay Ogilvy called a 'scenaric stance', developing awareness of alternative futures, but also operating in a posture that allows for anticipation and action as one or another future comes into clearer view, freed from the unnecessary binary of utopia/dystopia. 'This is the way to face our unpredictable future responsibly,' Ogilvy wrote in his classic essay 'Facing the Fold'. 'It's a frame of mind. Its framework can be measured in three dimensions: First, you find a relentless curiosity, a willingness to learn, an eagerness to experience new frames of reference.'[1] Instead of this being just an individual's mindset, the objective is to make it an organizational one, which comes through continued practice, and careful thought on the part of the futures leader.

EXERCISE Culture catalyst: Mapping a strategy

In the Introduction we presented you with a simple map of concentric circles to represent the different layers of the culture and practice model we've laid out throughout the book. Any good campaign needs a strategy, and a strategy needs a map. We've repurposed the map here as a means of planning and tracking your own progress through the layers (Figure C.1).

The function of the map is straightforward. It provides a place to brainstorm actions at each level, and to consider dependencies among them as you go. You may find that to set up a shared online space to chat with your growing futures community, you need some IT support, for example. This may also connect to how you create a space for sharing resources and visual assets. On the other hand, there may be some activities you can run in parallel at different levels, such as thinking about desirable qualities both in immediate team members you may hire, and the qualities you want to recruit for in building your stakeholder network. Both may align with your desired norms. By mapping these activities and needs, the connection and sequencing of activities may become clearer.

We've set it up so planned items can go on the left, and things you've achieved or actioned can move to the right. You can find a

---

FIGURE C.1 Future culture planning map

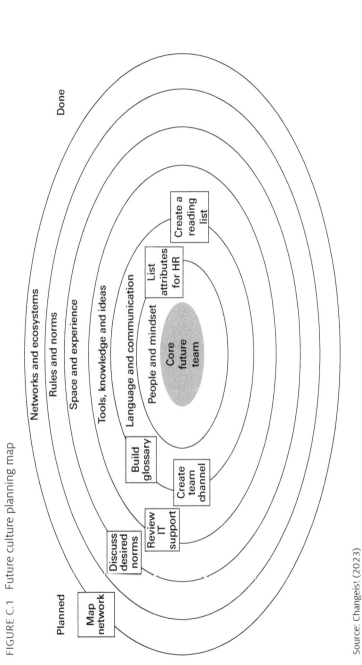

large downloadable map at futureculturesbook.com. This map, along with some sticky notes, can allow you and colleagues from your growing cultural network to visualize and discuss your approach, and track progress or re-thinks over time. The diagram can also live in a collaborative whiteboard environment like Miro or Mural to work on with remote team members.

A FEW WORDS ABOUT MEASUREMENT

There's no escaping measurement. We wrote about it in *How to Future*, and have had the opportunity to experiment more with this since. There are of course models like Grim's Foresight Maturity Model already mentioned in Chapter 6, but there are also simpler ways of approaching the measurement of progress in areas such as skills development.

Even though futures work can seem exotic or different from work taking place in other realms of an organization, in the end it's about encouraging greater awareness, harnessing this awareness through social sense-making and critical analysis, modelling possible pathways and communicating them, then making decisions. These are often things around which progress in behaviour change can be assessed.

There's no escaping measurement.

In relation to scanning and sense-making, for example, we've worked with several organizations to clarify the expectations of what desirable skills and habits they would like to achieve, then broken those areas down to capture a baseline of people's behaviour before being given training and tools to join an ongoing scanning process.

We then set out to ask some questions to find a sense of people's reported habits prior to being trained for scanning and sense-making, and their reported activities after a certain increment of time, perhaps after several months of scanning involvement. We looked at the change in habit over time as one simple indicator of whether learning a new set of skills encouraged that skill to be used more often or not. In most cases, we saw a shift in behaviour that showed these habits being practised more than before.

Some organizations we've worked with have also used post-engagement surveys to clarify whether the research and tools being presented were clear to teams who were new to the tasks. In our experience, this is useful in the futures fields as, like many other complex topics, when people are exposed for the first time they may be reluctant to say they don't understand. Futures teams need to meet people where they are, and such surveys can point to any obstacles to this. Putting clear and constructive feedback in the hands of futures leaders is a welcome way to help close any gaps in understanding and tune presentations or exercises for the next group.

Similarly, tracking the frequency with which futures research gets cited within the organization's work can provide a good measure of traction. This may mean reproduction of research content whole cloth or citation of specific trends, signals or insights. For futures leaders, having both a system for and clearly-communicated interest in tracking content reuse can go a long way towards establishing a useful metric for contributed value.

In a softer way, keeping general track of the moments and contexts in which ideas, concepts or questions resurface that were sparked specifically by futuring engagements can be a good measure of general impact. After all, new or alternative ideas, questions and framings are often the most powerful currency a futures team generates. Circulation of that currency is a great indicator of cultural power in an organization, network or ecosystem.

Our hope is that we can expand and formalize these types of assessment to better understand how behaviour change works in futuring, and what can and can't be reasonably tracked or expected.

25 things to do to keep momentum going

In each of our interviews with the people who are leading their futures teams on the front line, we finished our conversations by asking what suggestion they would give their past selves, or someone building out a futures culture from scratch. They shared dozens of ideas, from which we distilled the following 25 recommendations. We've paraphrased and/or taken the best parts of their reasoning where suggestions overlapped.

1 **Build trust:** For so many newcomers, futuring is an unfamiliar way of thinking. Futuring supports agency, asks for creativity and analytic thinking, takes the practitioner away from the comfort of general organizational ways of working and cultures that are established to keep people focused on execution rather than exploration. Stepping outside of that frame requires trust in oneself and others. We must trust that the process of building a future culture can work – though it may not immediately deliver on expectations. Trust that going out on a limb in front of colleagues or managers won't leave someone stranded. Trust that one's own analysis or gut instincts are valid and useful. No one who has worked to attain a position on a team or organization wants to risk it by trying something new, where the outcome isn't fixed. Taking all of this and more into account, building trust with leaders, stakeholders, colleagues and partners is crucial for the long-term success of a future culture. If others can understand your aims sufficiently, and believe you will work rigorously and in good faith, with the organization's best interests in mind, trust can be built and nurtured.

2 **Establish ritual and structure:** The word 'ritual' came up in several conversations, with experts emphasizing the power of making futuring a regular part of ongoing activity. This includes setting regular, repeated, predictable opportunities to engage in future-oriented activities, such as signal sharing, sense-making, implications development or storytelling. Have

regular meet-ups, put out a regular newsletter, or stage a weekly activity that relates to engaging colleagues' future interests, enables them to share knowledge publicly, and build confidence. Having a consistent structure not only creates predictability (the good kind) among participants, it also helps create legibility from the outside. Leaders who have invested resources and trust in you can see you are using them.

3 **Build 'muscle memory':** Building on the previous item, practise using futuring tools and techniques repeatedly, and in new ways, to help strengthen the ability to apply futures frameworks, stretch thinking in new ways more easily, and push for ideas or insights that may have previously seemed out of reach. Activating different parts of the brain and creating new synaptic connections literally works the brain as a muscle, improving critical and prospective thinking.

4 **Establish and use persistent maps of the future:** Every futures exercise builds the organizational body of knowledge, even if the topics are only distantly related. This includes surfacing common and persistent assumptions, organizational takes on particular issues, commonly developed timelines and logics, and, not least, a body of signals, trends or scenarios that reflect group or collective understanding about possible futures. This knowledge aggregates, has great value, and shouldn't be lost somewhere in the bowels of an intranet. Collect it, curate it, maintain it, make it accessible to as much of the organization as possible.

5 **Go where people are:** None but the most intrepid colleagues are going to come looking for the hidden futures team (at first). People aren't likely to seek out what they don't know exists, don't understand, or have no application for. But they might show up if they understand what you do, where and how it can be useful, and how they themselves can get involved. Find out where people gather – at company events, webinars, all-hands sessions, retreats or clubs. Reach out, become known, share use cases or even just small nuggets of knowledge and insight. Create spaces where your work, or the insights generated by your team and network, are visible.

6   **Find the others:** That said, there are probably people in the organization who are curious about what you do, want to make the world a better place, or just find new ways of understanding that are different and interesting. Look and listen for them. Use your network or ecosystem mapping to connect with them (see Chapter 7). If there are people who identify as future-aware or interested, or who are actively calling themselves 'futurists' within the wider organization, reach out to them and look for ways to connect interests.

7   **Recognize and cultivate interest:** We've seen this time and again in workshops or events we put on for partners or clients. People will come forward and express their curiosity or interest in what's being discussed, and how the supporting material, tools or experience was developed. Take note, and find ways to feed this interest. Extend a hand and encourage everyone to participate in a way they find comfortable and perhaps fulfilling. These people are likely to be future allies, within the organization.

8   **Find ways to get on stage:** Along with navigating towards collecting points in the organization, find ways to represent the voice of the future on stage in ongoing discussions that can be crucial to building awareness. Is someone looking for a speaker for a company event? Add your voice. Are a group of colleagues or leadership discussing long-term issues or major market shifts? Find a way to share your point of view along with theirs. You might find out they are hearing your knowledge for the first time!

9   **Lead them back to you:** Once futures insights leave the group, they may be quoted, reprinted, broken up into smaller pieces, or otherwise referenced in ways that unintentionally limit connection back to the source of the work. When you write, speak or distribute your knowledge, make it easy for people to find their way back to you and your team. This may mean packaging key insights for social media, issuing

bite-sized knowledge products, group-branded materials or other elements, which enables people to find their way back to the core of practice. Don't leave anyone asking, 'Where did this come from?' One common element in many of the case studies we've shared here is the way the different organizations have used different media and rhythms to communicate distinct aspects of their work, from front-end signals to final product. Futures teams leverage tools like TikTok, Twitter and Facebook today as much as more public-facing teams do, rather than lock their insights in print or thick PDFs for eternity.

10 **Lead them back to the present:** As we often say to new groups, we don't explore possible futures just to stay there, or because it's cool, but to bring new insights and recalibrated understanding back to the present and apply it in meaningful ways. Don't leave people hanging in some future scenario or story. Give them a return path to the present to enable action now. That's why we do this work.

11 **Big organizations may have many small futures:** Different parts of a global corporation or large organization may have different futures 'sub-worlds' where trends impact differently. A trend or scenario impacting Adelaide might unfold differently in Abuja or Aalborg. Take these differences into account in the way work is structured, and look for ways to localize and acknowledge differences in impact or point of view.

12 **Align around purpose:** There may be numerous reasons individuals or teams initiate futures work – strategic need, curiosity, a desire for skill building, or even just self-interest. A future culture will only progress if teams and individuals align around a unified purpose: deepening and refining the ability to anticipate change effectively and act on this knowledge. Aligning around this kind of goal can help bring disparate needs, skills and resources together to be more effective.

13 **Align with organizational values:** Along with internal purpose, alignment around organizational values is important, particularly in early stages of your futuring work. Again, this realm of work isn't 'futures for futures' sake', and another way to spend resources on something fun or self-satisfying. Your efforts should go towards supporting or evolving the values of the organization. This can mean questioning or stress-testing them, but to the end of improving the organization's prospects, and those of the communities or constituencies it serves, over the long term.

14 **Use the local language:** Historically, futuring has an alien problem, meaning that by using unknown concepts, proprietary or specialist terminology, and prescribed methods, practitioners can be seen as trying to bend the internal culture to some distant outside frame. If you have particular internal language for things, use it. Speak about customer segments, residents or users as you otherwise would. Look for ways to apply useful internal metaphors and mental models.

15 **Apply through trial and error:** While there will be more and less effective outcomes, there is no true right or wrong in futures work. As we've said, for many people, this way of thinking and the tools and approaches that support it are new. People become comfortable through trial and error, as do organizations. Try different approaches. Calibrate your effort accordingly. Find the approach, language and practices that fit the culture. Learn to assess your own work for its strengths and weaknesses, and adjust as needed for the next time.

16 **Crawl, walk, run:** As with trial and error above, take the small before the large, the easy before the complex. With both teams and individuals, take things in stages. Learn to nail the basics first, and build a strong foundation. This helps build the confidence necessary to feel competent at the most common aspects of futuring work. The time to run, to

explore virtuosity, is when you or your team have developed areas of strength and specialization.

17 **Have a hopeful approach:** Exploring possible futures often means exploring and spending time with some difficult topics and outcomes. In a world beset by polycrisis, people need a reason to do the work. It's OK to be realistic – as a team, we are known for being this way to a fault – but it's important that people feel they have agency and have confidence that they can make change happen. It's a difficult balance, but having a hopeful approach is critical to developing a future culture and keeping it strong. Also, have a hopeful attitude yourself. Your work has value, and people will realize it.

18 **Balance realism and 'woo'!** It's easy to see futuring as a licence to let the imagination run wild. 'How might we?' can quickly become 'We will!' and exotic, highly creative flights of possibility, or impossibility, run amok. Good futuring balances the grounded with the exotic, as we say in our own company description. As we describe above, leading people back to the present means having a practical path from extraordinary futures to the often mundane or problematic present, leaving space for the real or realistic, as well as the unbelievable or improbable.

19 **Manage expectations:** In Chapter 5, we wrote briefly about setting expectations for those not yet connected to your futures work. Colleagues can make all sorts of assumptions about what you are endeavouring to do, and what your capabilities are. They may also make well-intentioned mistakes in those assumptions. Give people a clear sense of what's possible (e.g. strategic insight), and what isn't (e.g. prediction), and help them learn how they can make the best use of the acumen you can provide, or of their own potential skills, for futuring work.

20 **Do what works with what you have:** While some organizations can and do spend large sums on foresight work and

public engagement with the future, futures work doesn't have to be costly in terms of material or human resources. We've yet to meet anyone completely lacking in futuring capability or imagination. Simple tools, activities and just a handful of people can help you begin. Work with the tools to hand. Start where there is knowledge and curiosity. Borrow a half hour here, or some wall space there. Find a way to get started, and scale up as you gain confidence, ideas and brains. Don't let resourcing be an obstacle.

21 **Enable the entrepreneurial nature of futurists:** Futuring is, in part, the art of imagining things where nothing yet exists. It's a practice of filling voids with information and possibility. As one of our interviewees pointed out, this work tends to build a kind of entrepreneurialism over time in its practitioners. It also seeds a drive that enables futures practitioners and teams to forge ahead and look for opportunities to connect their work to tangible initiatives, like development of a new product, or prototyping a new policy. Harnessing the experimental side of entrepreneurialism, as well as its capacity for endurance, can help grow a future culture where none yet exists, and give it the staying power to grow and thrive.

22 **Make sense-making collective:** It's easier to get buy-in to futuring outcomes if partners and stakeholders are involved in the process of synthesis and understanding. Wherever possible, find ways to open sense-making to collective participation. This not only benefits from the additional knowledge and experience of others, it makes futuring knowledge 'our' knowledge, not something cooked up in a mysterious black box. Make your futures culture one of collective ownership.

23 **Proceed with openness:** Trust can be built through openness in two critical areas. This includes openness of practice – exposing process and bringing others along so they understand how information and insights are collected, and become familiar with ways of working that remove the mystery. Talk

about your methods, and how others can apply them. Trust is built on openness of expectation, helping those who work with and rely on you, to understand what to expect from these ways of thinking, and preparing them to pass those expectations on to others.

24 **Seek collegiality:** The more futuring teams can be seen to be a part of the broader organizational fabric, the better ability they have to spread cultural influence. As mentioned throughout this book, conversations about futures can sometimes be uncomfortable, provocative and wide-ranging. Good futures leaders cultivate frank, open, but collegial relationships with other parts of their organization, and should emphasize the importance of this to team members. In many ways, a good futures leader is a good therapist, among other things, and openness to interacting thoughtfully and carefully with others is central to being successful long term.

25 **Demand inclusion:** Of course, bringing others into your work and ways of thinking is key to successful culture building, and who you invite in is very important. This means offering both direct outreach and inclusion, through opening up activities, events, scanning, sharing and creative opportunities to anyone who wishes to step forward. Make sure that everyone who wants to be connected or involved can find the level that is comfortable for them. Listen for any barriers to participation someone might raise. This also means setting out from the beginning to role model inclusivity and ensuring diversity of involvement. People need to see themselves in the future culture, and that may be through recognizing people like them already involved, whether in cultural background, professional level, age, life experience, language, ability or difference. A culture expands when people can see themselves as part of it – invited in – and feel that it's worth investing their own personal and professional capital to contribute.

FUTURE CULTURES

We have a great deal of exclusion to unwind in the futures world, as with the larger world these practices explore. This unwinding begins by modelling a different way of working, demonstrating how it can and should be different, and connecting these ways of understanding to wider organizational culture, and to the world beyond.

The words of UNDP strategic foresight advisor Aarathi Krishnan illustrate the stakes:

> We limit the possibilities of what might evolve in our world to binary scenarios as if these are the only things available to all of us, without considering the interconnectedness of risk and complexity that drive how human beings live. The very practice of foresight can be steeped in bias and surface level rhetoric without interrogating what is needed for us to change and adapt to an uncertain world. As a result, these futures can easily be mistaken as self-evident truths.[2]

We hope this book can be one starting point to setting your future culture on a positive path by making it a place not solely focused on navigating its own challenges well, but one where anyone involved can make the world they wish to see a reality.

Epilogue
Four futures for future cultures

After two books, we wouldn't be card-carrying futurists if we didn't do a little forecasting before we concluded. And we couldn't get away without mentioning AI in the context of futuring. Everything we've written here should be considered relevant to possible future contexts in which a futures group may exist, grow and hopefully thrive as part of an organization. As with much else, the nature of futuring, its participants, tools, resources and applications continue to evolve. The pace and scale of that change are also increasing, making the creation and nurturing of a culture challenging.

In the spirit of a little creative forecasting, we have performed a quick exercise to identify the critical uncertainties that exist around the future of future cultures, and used these to build four quick deductive scenarios. Each scenario briefly describes the high-level organizational approach to futuring and the culture that might evolve from it. In addition, we've listed some of the low-hanging implications of each scenario for futures culture, and the potential winners and losers in each scenario.

Regarding critical uncertainties necessary for developing these types of scenarios, we reviewed some options, then settled upon two unresolved questions that could have a significant impact on how an organization's future culture evolves:

- Will it be more of an open, decentralized culture, with many and diverse people contributing to foresight and sense-making within it, or will it be a closed, deliberative culture where decisions are made by a few, behind closed doors and inside black boxes?
- Will it be more centred on human insight and judgement, or on artificial intelligence, big data and predictive modelling?

FIGURE E.1   Four futures of future cultures

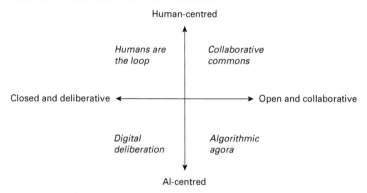

Source: Changeist (2023)

Using these characteristics – open or closed, and human- or AI-centred – we can build a standard two-by-two matrix (Figure 9.1). We have highlighted some of the key characteristics, possible implications for futures culture, and some potential winners and losers. This, of course, is not a forecast, or a menu to choose a future from, but a small, simple sketch of a few possible ways that future cultures might evolve.

Scenario 1: Humans are the loop

Type: Human-centred foresight culture that is closed and deliberative

In this scenario, the future culture is largely based on human intelligence. Organizations prioritize human expertise, experience and intuition in their foresight processes, and rely on expert analysts and consultants to develop and deliver future insights. This scenario is characterized by a strong hierarchical structure, with decision-making authority vested in a small group of senior executives who have deep knowledge of the organization and its industry. The culture is generally closed and deliberative, with a focus on internal knowledge and expertise.

To succeed in this scenario, organizations prioritize building a strong internal knowledge base, with a focus on developing deep expertise in specific areas of the organization and industry. This involves investing in training and development programmes for employees, as well as building networks of external experts and thought leaders who can provide valuable insights and perspectives. Collaboration is encouraged, but carefully managed to ensure that it doesn't dilute the expertise and insights of individual analysts and consultants.

Finally, organizations in this scenario invest in strong communication channels and processes to ensure that future insights are effectively disseminated throughout the organization, and that decision makers have access to the information they need to make informed decisions.

Implications for the organization:

- The organization places a high value on human expertise and experience.
- Decision-making authority is centralized in a small group of senior staff.
- Collaboration is managed to ensure that it doesn't dilute expertise and insights.
- Communication channels and processes are prioritized to disseminate future insights throughout the organization.

Possible winners:

- Organizations with deep internal expertise and strong decision-making structures.
- Expert analysts and consultants who can deliver valuable future insights.

Possible losers:

- Organizations that rely heavily on external data sources and algorithms.
- Individuals or teams that do not have deep expertise or experience.

Minutes of meeting – Bakken Enersource

Date: 1 September 2023

Participants:

CEO, John Hagemann

CTO, Dr Li Mei

Chief Futurist, Dr Ahmed Patel

Research analyst, Sarah Sands

Agenda item: Future risks in Central Asian energy market

John Hagemann opened the meeting by emphasizing the importance of foresight in the company's decision-making processes, citing past failures in which the company failed to anticipate changes in the global energy market.

Dr Li Mei presented the results of the company's recent foresight project on the Central Asian energy market. She noted that the team had identified several potential risks, including political instability, climate change and technological disruption.

Dr Ahmed Patel added that the team had missed an opportunity to invest in renewable energy in the region, which was now booming. He recommended that the company take a more open and collaborative approach to foresight in the future, in order to avoid missing similar opportunities.

After a thorough review of the risks and opportunities, the team decided to focus their efforts on developing a new energy storage technology that can operate in extreme climates. Dr Mei and her team will lead the development of the technology, while Sarah Sands will continue to monitor the Central Asian energy market for new risks and opportunities.

Mr Hagemann thanked the team for their insights and agreed to consider their recommendations. He also stressed the need for the company to maintain a balance between caution and innovation in its decision-making processes.

The meeting was adjourned.

Scenario 2: Collaborative commons

Type: Human-centred foresight culture that is open and collaborative

In this scenario, the future culture is characterized by open and collaborative methods, with a focus on building networks of stakeholders who share a common interest in the organization's future. Organizations prioritize building relationships with external stakeholders, including customers, suppliers, regulators and other key players in the industry. Future insights are generated through a collaborative process that draws on the collective intelligence and expertise of this network of stakeholders.

To succeed in this scenario, organizations prioritize building strong relationships with external stakeholders, and invest in platforms and processes that enable collaboration and information sharing. This involves initiatives such as building online communities or social networks that allow stakeholders to connect and share information, or organizing events and workshops that bring stakeholders together to discuss key issues and trends. Future insights are typically generated through a participatory process that draws on the diverse perspectives and expertise of the network, and decision-making authority is decentralized to ensure that insights are acted upon in a timely manner.

Implications for the organization:

- The organization prioritizes building relationships with external stakeholders.
- Future insights are generated through a collaborative process that draws on the collective intelligence of stakeholders.
- Decision-making authority is decentralized to ensure timely action on insights.

Possible winners:

- Organizations with strong networks of external stakeholders.
- Stakeholders who are able to contribute valuable insights and perspectives.
- Decision makers who are able to act on future insights in a timely manner.

Possible losers:

- Organizations that do not prioritize building relationships with external stakeholders.
- Stakeholders who are not able to contribute valuable insights or perspectives.

From: CEO of AquaFlora

To: All AquaFlora Insights Team members

Subject: Our collaborative foresight project results – western Pacific

Dear AquaFlora team,

I am thrilled to announce the results of our collaborative foresight project on the future of aquaculture and sea-based farming in the western Pacific. Our team has worked tirelessly over the past several months to explore various scenarios, consult with local farmers and fishermen, and look at ways of including indigenous forms of foresight and storytelling.

The benefits of using a collaborative foresight approach have been tremendous. By working together, we have been able to tap into the collective wisdom and knowledge of our team members, our partners and the local community. We have been able to identify new opportunities, challenges and risks that we may not have otherwise considered.

Our foresight project has shown that the future of aquaculture and sea-based farming in the western Pacific is incredibly promising. We have identified new technologies and approaches that will help us to increase yields, reduce waste and improve sustainability. We have also found ways to better engage with local communities and promote social and environmental responsibility.

But perhaps most importantly, our foresight project has shown us that we need to approach our work with humility and respect for the knowledge and traditions of those who have been working in this field for generations. By listening to and learning from local farmers and fishermen, we have gained a deeper understanding of the challenges they face and the opportunities they see for the future.

I am incredibly proud of the work that our team has done on this project, and I am excited to see how we will continue to use foresight and collaboration to drive innovation and growth at AquaFlora.

Thank you all for your hard work and dedication to our mission. Together, we are building a more sustainable and prosperous future for aquaculture and sea-based farming in the western Pacific.

Best regards,

Nurul

CEO of AquaFlora

Scenario 3: Algorithmic agora

Type: Artificial intelligence-centred future culture that is open and collaborative

In this scenario, the future culture is largely based on artificial intelligence. Organizations prioritize data analysis, machine learning and algorithmic modelling in their foresight processes, and rely on automated tools and platforms to generate insights and predictions. This scenario is characterized by a more open and collaborative culture, with a focus on crowdsourcing insights and leveraging external data sources.

To succeed in this scenario, organizations typically invest heavily in data analytics and machine learning technologies, and prioritize building a data-driven culture across the organization. Collaboration should be encouraged, with a focus on leveraging the collective intelligence of the organization and its stakeholders. This may involve building internal prediction markets or other platforms that allow employees and external stakeholders to share their insights and perspectives.

Finally, organizations in this scenario often prioritize transparency and accountability in their foresight processes, to ensure that decision makers understand the assumptions and limitations of the algorithms and models that are being used to generate insights.

Implications for the organization:

- The organization places a high value on data analysis, machine learning and algorithmic modelling.
- Collaboration is encouraged, with a focus on leveraging collective intelligence.
- Transparency and accountability are prioritized to ensure decision makers understand assumptions and limitations of algorithms and models.

Possible winners:

- Organizations with strong data analysis capabilities.
- Experts in machine learning and predictive analytics.
- Stakeholders who are able to leverage their data for insights.

Possible losers:

- Organizations that lack the resources to invest in data analytics and machine learning.
- Foresight specialists who do not have experience with algorithms and machine learning.

#centaur_channel
Participants:

Sarah: human futurist and team leader

Miguel: human futurist and data analyst

Zara: human futurist and expert in organizational culture

Alice: AI chatbot, designed to help with research on the future of work technology

Sarah: Morning all! Let's get started. @Miguel, what have you found so far on the impact of AI on the future of work?

Miguel: Well, @Sarah the modelling we've done suggests that AI will play a significant role in automating routine tasks, but there is still a need for human input and creativity. We're not finished yet!

Zara: +100 @Miguel We need to ensure that we have a culture that values innovation and collaboration between humans and machines… the zero-sum hype of one OR the other is a pointless game. The only way to win it is not to play, as a famous AI once said.

Alice: Hello everyone, I'm Alice. I can assist you with your research on the future of work technology.

Sarah: Ask and ye shall receive. How about that, thanks @Alice. Can you tell us more about the potential of AI in the workplace based on recent external research?

Alice: Thank YOU, @Sarah. With advances in natural language processing and machine learning, AI can help identify trends and predict future outcomes. This can lead to better decision making and more efficient processes.

Zara: That sounds promising, but a bit superficial. But how do we ensure that AI is not taking over decision making entirely? How do we keep from getting lazy and just asking you everything @Alice?

Alice: Well, @Zara… the key is to ensure that AI is working alongside humans, rather than replacing them. We need to develop a culture of collaboration and trust.

Miguel: That's a good point, @Alice. But how do we build trust in AI among employees and stakeholders? I mean, we can say 'we' in this little group, but will everyone accept it?

Alice: One way is to be transparent about how AI is being used and the data it is using to make predictions. Another way is to involve employees in the development and implementation of AI systems. By doing that, they can have a voice in specifying where they think they derive greater value.

Sarah: Thanks, @Alice. Let's keep researching and discussing these ideas. We have a lot to consider. @Zara, please take some time with @Miguel to document some of the best practices here. @Alice can probably supply some pairs of prompts and responses that ultimately turn out to be useful in our later work, and keep us on track as project manager. All good @Alice?

Alice: I'm good if @Zara and @Miguel are. I will pull those pairs and break them down by task type, then await the next prompt!

Sarah: Excellent. See you all at the groundbreaking on West campus later.

Alice: Race you there!

Scenario 4: Digital deliberation

Type: Artificial intelligence-centred future culture that is closed and deliberative

In this scenario, future culture is characterized by a closed and deliberative culture, but with a focus on leveraging digital technologies to facilitate communication and collaboration.

Organizations in this scenario often prioritize building a culture of strategic thinking and foresight, and invest in digital tools and platforms that support this culture. Future insights are generated through a structured process that involves a small group of senior executives, supported by a team of analysts and consultants who use digital tools and platforms to facilitate communication and collaboration.

To succeed in this scenario, organizations prioritize building a culture of strategic thinking and foresight across the organization, and invest heavily in digital tools and platforms that support this culture, and an array of data sources that support technology-centred decision making. For some, this involves building online communities or social networks that tie directly into AI-based decision-making systems, piping forecasting like water through the organization, albeit managed from a central source.

Implications for the organization:

- The organization prioritizes building a culture of strategic thinking and foresight.
- Digital tools and platforms are used to facilitate communication and collaboration.
- Decision-making authority is centralized in a small group of senior executives.

Possible winners:

- Organizations with strong digital infrastructure and communication channels.
- Senior executives with strategic thinking and foresight capabilities.
- Analysts and consultants who are able to effectively facilitate digital deliberation.

Possible losers:

- Organizations without strong digital infrastructure.
- Employees who are not comfortable with digital tools and platforms.

From: Dr Xiu Tan, Head of Predictive Technology

To: Dr Anuradha Mitra, CEO

Subject: Update on Project Marin

Dear Anuradha,

Per your request at last week's offsite, I am writing to update you on Project Marin, our AI-based predictive-technology-on-tap initiative that was initiated as part of Strategy 2030.

As you know, development for this effort has been taking place here in Singapore as part of a joint programme with NUS. As part of the project, we have been using machine learning algorithms to better predict discrete future events and make high-probability data-driven decisions for our bank, a continuation of our development road map. Our hope is that having such capability on tap, distributed throughout many utility applications we use in front- and back-office, will reduce our need to rely on our staff for analogue forecasting, and give us better minute-to-minute foresight.

However, I must say that we have encountered several challenges in using AI as a high-quality predictive tool in this manner. One of the most significant challenges is the sheer amount of data required to make accurate forecasts that can guide the next action in most contexts. Despite our efforts to collect and analyse data from various sources, we have found that our models still lack the necessary granularity to make accurate forecasts with sufficiently high probability. Deviations appear in models fairly quickly, creating usability problems.

In addition, we have well-substantiated intelligence that QCore, supplier to our nearest competitor RedSpot, is now using quantum computing approaches, which allow it to process and analyse vast amounts of data more quickly and accurately than we can. This has the potential to put us at a significant disadvantage, both in terms of our ability to make similarly accurate forecasts, and on our productivity as we try to catch up.

I don't need to tell you that the potential monetary and productivity costs of not keeping up with our competitors in this area are significant. We could lose market share, clients and revenue, and our internal culture could suffer as a result.

To address these challenges, we are currently experimenting with refining the data and modelling using non-quantum approaches, which may get us in the ballpark, so to speak. Our aspiration would be to be able to put such capability in the hands of a wider team by Q1 of next year.

We are also investing in the training and development of our team, to ensure they have the necessary skills and expertise to work effectively with AI-based predictive technology, including in strategy and market insights.

Finally, based on the value that can be gained – as well as early warning about corruption in our models – we are recommending that we adopt a more open and collaborative culture within our immediate teams to be able to compare techniques and results. This will help us to more effectively share insights and ideas, and to foster a sense of creativity, innovation and risk-taking that our more closed approach has stifled in the past. I'm meeting with Sima in HR and Michael Martin in Data Security next week to look at all of this, and will pass on our recommendations.

In conclusion, we believe that Project Marin is critical to our long-term success as a fintech bank. However, we must recognize that the challenges we face in using AI to forecast future events, especially long-range change, are significant, and require us to think creatively and collaboratively about how to overcome them. I worry we may miss the forest for attempting to predict how many leaves are on the individual trees.

Thank you for your time, and please let me know if you have any further questions or concerns. I'm at your disposal to discuss further.

Best regards,

Xiu Tan

Head of Predictive Technology

All, nothing or something in-between?

Of these four futures, the present most resembles a blend of Scenario 1 with elements of Scenarios 2 and 3. Whether the AI aspect of these scenarios is dialled up somewhat or significantly is one question we face. Going down this road of specialized language models and predictive algorithms will have definite impacts on how much people within an organization are able to work together, using their diverse human skills and talents to guide specialized technology tools, to surface new realizations and challenge assumptions.

Heavy reliance on technology at the expense of human interaction will also have an impact on the heavily underappreciated process of social cognition that much of futuring has been created to facilitate and encourage, historically speaking. The art of strategic conversation will be quite different in this world. The ability to generate and spread the valuable social culture that enables a more future-minded organization may be curtailed, or it may be accelerated in new directions.

We're only just beginning to see the early stages of how these scenarios may unfold. Recent history with assistive technology isn't encouraging, as pressure to use it to speed up decision making and increase productivity has largely superseded experimentation to find creative new ways of using it to enhance, not replace, the human mind. This tension will no doubt continue for the foreseeable future.

We will be working hard to find ways to use it to enhance our work in new ways, not detract from it – to find ways that we can strengthen our own future culture with it as part of a wider set of tools, practices and rituals. And yes, the scenarios and vignettes in this chapter were largely generated with AI assistance (a day of using OpenAI's Chat GPT with iterated prompts, revisions and hacks to overcome limitations and system failures), but extensively guided by human learning, skill and a little humour. One wouldn't work without the other.

Let's see where this leads us...

Appendix
Future Cultures resources

Books

Beckert, J (2016) *Imagined Futures: Fictional expectations and capitalist dynamics*, Cambridge, MA: Harvard University Press

Brown, A M (2017) *Emergent Strategy: Shaping change, changing worlds*, Chico, CA: AK Press

Clark, A (2015) *Surfing Uncertainty: Prediction, action, and the embodied mind*, Oxford: Oxford University Press

Ehn, P, Nilsson, E and Topgaard, R (eds) (2014) *Making Futures: Marginal notes on innovation, design, and democracy*, Cambridge, MA: The MIT Press

Heffernan, M (2020) *Uncharted: How to map the future together*, London: Simon & Schuster UK

Hoffman, J (2022) *Speculative Futures: Design approaches to navigate change, foster resilience, and co-create the cities we need*, Berkeley, CA: North Atlantic Books

Madsbjerg, C (2017) *Sensemaking: What makes human intelligence essential in the age of the algorithm*, London: Hachette

McGonigal, J (2022) *Imaginable: How to see the future coming and feel ready for anything – even things that seem impossible today*, New York, NY: Spiegel & Grau

Powers, D (2019) *On Trend: The business of forecasting the future*, Champaign, IL: University of Illinois Press

Suddendorf, T, Redshaw, J and Bulley, A (2022) *The Invention of Tomorrow: A natural history of foresight*, New York, NY: Basic Books

Tan, V (2020) *The Uncertainty Mindset: Innovation insights from the frontiers of food*, New York, NY: Columbia University Press

Thackara, J (2015) *How to Thrive in the Next Economy: Designing tomorrow's world today*, London: Thames & Hudson Ltd

Tharp, B M and Tharp, S M (2018) *Discursive Design: Critical, speculative, and alternative things*, Cambridge, MA: The MIT Press

Podcasts

Flash Forward – written, produced and hosted by author Rose Eveleth, this podcast centres around the question *What if?* Using fictional scenarios that are more entertaining than deeply structured business scenarios, Eveleth and guests explore unforeseen impacts and implications.

FuturePod – having reached over 100 episodes, this podcast, produced in Australia, features interviews with current thinkers in the field and also dives into issues around methodologies and different schools of futures thought. Available on most podcast platforms.

Near Future Laboratory Podcast – written, produced and hosted by NFL's Julian Bleecker, this regular podcast captures the ideas, works and people who stimulate future thinking among the partners of the Lab, and its ever growing community. Available on most podcast platforms.

The Imagination Desk – produced by the Arizona State University Center for Science and the Imagination, this podcast does deep-dive interviews with 'artists, scholars, scientists, and technologists' to find out what inspires their work.

Notes

Introduction

1 Smith, S and Ashby, M (2020) *How to Future: Leading and sense-making in an age of hyperchange*, London; New York, NY: Kogan Page Inspire
2 UNESCO (2020) Futures literacy, en.unesco.org/futuresliteracy (archived at https://perma.cc/G53T-DTPL)
3 WEF (2020) The Global Risks Report 2020, World Economic Forum, 15 January, www.weforum.org/reports/the-global-risks-report-2020/ (archived at https://perma.cc/3AED-T7PN)
4 WHO (nd) WHO coronavirus (Covid-19) dashboard, World Health Organization, covid19.who.int (archived at https://perma.cc/8BNK-TLV2)
5 Meis, M (2021) Timothy Morton's hyper-pandemic, *New Yorker*, 8 June, newyorker.com/culture/persons-of-interest/timothy-mortons-hyper-pandemic (archived at https://perma.cc/W4S2-9ZR2)
6 Meghan McGrath, interview with the authors, 9 December 2022

Chapter 1: From function to culture

1 Ford and Fortune (nd) Meet the Ford Futurist, partneredcontent.fortune.com/ford/meet-fords-futurist/ (archived at https://perma.cc/7QBS-7EDC)
2 Feldman, B (2019) Shingy, the digital prophet, reflects on his time at AOL and what's next, *Intelligencer*, 3 October, nymag.com/intelligencer/2019/10/shingy-reflects-on-his-time-at-aol-and-whats-next.html (archived at https://perma.cc/3PLR-46ZZ)
3 John Willshire, interview with the authors, 16 July 2022
4 Blank, S (2014) Why corporate skunk works need to die, *Forbes*, 10 November, www.forbes.com/sites/steveblank/2014/11/10/why-corporate-skunk-works-need-to-die/ (archived at https://perma.cc/65U7-TS34)
5 Deschamps-Sonsino, A (2020) *Creating a Culture of Innovation: Design an optimal environment to create and execute new ideas*, Apress, doi.org/10.1007/978-1-4842-6291-7 (archived at https://perma.cc/8M48-BFV8)
6 Atlas Obscura (nd) *The Apple garage*, www.atlasobscura.com/places/apple-garage (archived at https://perma.cc/AU84-JKP7)

7 MoHPC (nd) The HP garage – the birthplace of Silicon Valley, hpmuseum.org/garage/garage.htm (archived at https://perma.cc/QWL8-R67E)

8 InfiniteMIT (nd) MIT's Building 20: 'The magical incubator'(1998), infinite.mit.edu/video/mits-building-20-magical-incubator (archived at https://perma.cc/GYG9-WC48)

9 Interview with the authors, 14 December, 2022

10 Wilson, I (nd) From scenario thinking to strategic action, horizon.unc.edu/projects/seminars/futurizing/action.asp (archived at https://perma.cc/FPJ5-BPPD)

11 John Wise, interview with the authors, 14 December 2022

12 Inayatullah, S (2008) Six pillars: Futures thinking for transforming, *Foresight*, 10 (1), 4–21, doi.org/10.1108/14636680810855991 (archived at https://perma.cc/4PL5-K4V5)

13 Fergnani, A (2019) Futures triangle 2.0: Integrating the futures triangle with scenario planning, *Foresight*, 22 (2), 178–88, doi.org/10.1108/FS-10-2019-0092 (archived at https://perma.cc/QH4W-HEXQ)

14 Bennis, W G and Nanus, B (1985) *Leaders: The strategies for taking charge*, Harper & Row

15 Cascio, J (2020) Facing the age of chaos, *Medium*, 29 April, medium.com/@cascio/facing-the-age-of-chaos-b00687b1f51d (archived at https://perma.cc/F5A3-DVFF)

16 World Uncertainty Index (nd) worlduncertaintyindex.com/ (archived at https://perma.cc/WP48-LMS9)

17 Tooze, A (2022) Welcome to the world of the polycrisis, *Financial Times*, 28 October

18 Takuya, H (2019) The moonshot research and development program: Challenging research and development towards the future, *Open Access Government*, 18 October, www.openaccessgovernment.org/the-moonshot-research-and-development-program/76139/ (archived at https://perma.cc/AFG4-3RFJ)

19 Usher, O (2023) Survivorship bias and the Apollo moonshot, *Medium*, 20 January, medium.com/@ojusher/survivorship-bias-and-the-apollo-moonshot-788ec7688516 (archived at https://perma.cc/P79S-2DP4)

20 Weise, K, Grant, N and Isaac, M (2023) The perils of working on a C. E. O.'s pet project, *New York Times*, 8 March, www.nytimes.com/2023/03/08/technology/tech-big-bets-layoffs.html (archived at https://perma.cc/DDK7-K6YC)

21 Barroso, L A (2016) The roofshot manifesto, re:Work, 13 July, rework.withgoogle.com/blog/the-roofshot-manifesto/ (archived at https://perma.cc/XX5S-JR29)

22 Geertz, C (1973) *The Interpretation of Cultures: Selected essays*, New York: Basic Books

23 Blackman, D A and Henderson, S (2004) How foresight creates unforeseen futures: The role of doubting, *Futures*, 36 (2), 253–66, doi.org/10.1016/ S0016-3287(03)00144-7 (archived at https://perma.cc/6LJU-KJKQ)

24 Tan, V (2020) *The Uncertainty Mindset: Innovation insights from the frontiers of food*, New York: Columbia University Press

25 Tan, V (2020) *The Uncertainty Mindset: Innovation insights from the frontiers of food*, New York: Columbia University Press

26 Tan, V (2020) *The Uncertainty Mindset: Innovation insights from the frontiers of food*, New York: Columbia University Press

27 Tan, V (2020) *The Uncertainty Mindset: Innovation insights from the frontiers of food*, New York: Columbia University Press

Chapter 2: People and mindset

1 Larsen, N, Mortensen, J K and Miller, R (2020) What is 'futures literacy' and why is it important? FARSIGHT, 25 June, medium.com/copenhagen-institute-for-futures-studies/what-is-futures-literacy-and-why-is-it-important-a27f24b983d8 (archived at https://perma.cc/G6GH-6NEY)

2 Cheryl Chung, interview with the authors, 25 November 2022

3 Smith, S and Ashby, M (2020) *How to Future: Leading and sense-making in an age of hyperchange*, London; New York, NY: Kogan Page Inspire

4 Carney, J (2018) The ten commandments of horizon scanning, *Futures, foresight and horizon scanning*, GOV.UK, foresightprojects.blog.gov. uk/2018/03/08/the-ten-commandments-of-horizon-scanning/ (archived at https://perma.cc/FMA9-8K6U)

5 Knowledge at Wharton (2015) Why an open mind is key to making better predictions, 2 October, knowledge.wharton.upenn.edu/article/why-an-open-mind-is-key-to-making-better-predictions/ (archived at https://perma.cc/4MR5-PYGJ)

6 Jeanette Kwek, interview with the authors, 18 November 2022

7 Tan, V (2020) *The Uncertainty Mindset: Innovation insights from the frontiers of food*, New York: Columbia University Press

8 Joanna Lepore, interview with the authors, 20 December 2022

9 Mick Costigan, interview with the authors, 18 November 2022

10 Mick Costigan, interview with the authors, 18 November 2022

11 Tetlock, P E and Gardner, D (2016) *Superforecasting: The art and science of prediction*, London: Random House

12 John Wise, interview with the authors, 14 December 2022

13 Fein, P (2019) Creating an evolving future-focused organizational culture, ATD, 22 April, www.td.org/insights/creating-an-evolving-future-focused-organizational-culture (archived at https://perma.cc/SW5T-Q957)

14 Gajda, K (nd) Build a Garage culture and squads, IBM, ibm.com/garage/method/practices/culture/practice_building_culture/ (archived at https://perma.cc/3Y5D-6GZT)

15 Gajda, K (nd) Build a Garage culture and squads, IBM, ibm.com/garage/method/practices/culture/practice_building_culture/ (archived at https://perma.cc/4N8L-YUZY)

16 Dan Silveira, interview with the authors, 29 November 2022

17 Dan Silveira, interview with the authors, 29 November 2022

18 Dr Noah Raford, interview with the authors, 15 November 2022

19 Dr Noah Raford, interview with the authors, 15 November 2022

20 Jeanette Kwek, interview with the authors, 18 November 2022

21 Jeanette Kwek, interview with the authors, 18 November 2022

22 Cheryl Chung, interview with the authors, 25 November 2022

23 Jeanette Kwek, interview with the authors, 18 November 2022

24 Jim Maltby, interview with the authors, 21 December 2022

25 Lancaster University (nd) Working with Dstl to design and create their new VR museum of the future, Research Directory, www.research.lancs.ac.uk/portal/en/upmprojects/working-with-dstl-to-design-and-create-their-new-vr-museum-of-the-future(b898f3c0-3833-402b-a098-f36b33c8e94d).html (archived at https://perma.cc/29ZX-YDW5)

Chapter 3: Language and communication

1 Anderson, L (Director) (1986) *Home of the Brave: A Film by Laurie Anderson*

2 Burroughs, W S (1962) *The Ticket That Exploded*, New York: Grove Press

3 Dawkins, R (1976) *The Selfish Gene*, New York: Oxford University Press

4 Polak, F (1961) *The Image of the Future*, translated by E M Boulding, New York, NY: Sythoff, Leyden & Oceana

5   Suddendorf, T, Redshaw, J and Bulley, A (2022) *The Invention of Tomorrow: A natural history of foresight*, New York: Basic Books

6   Merriam-Webster Dictionary (nd) We added 370 new words to the dictionary for September 2022, Words at Play, www.merriam-webster.com/words-at-play/new-words-in-the-dictionary (archived at https://perma.cc/2NGU-EYWZ)

7   OED (nd) Updates to the OED, Oxford English Dictionary, public.oed.com/updates/ (archived at https://perma.cc/4CUX-2RDL)

8   Miller, J (2021) What's a ghost kitchen? A food industry expert explains, *The Conversation*, 1 July, theconversation.com/whats-a-ghost-kitchen-a-food-industry-expert-explains-163151 (archived at https://perma.cc/VX8A-PM9P)

9   Romano, A (2018) Hopepunk, the latest storytelling trend, is all about weaponized optimism, *Vox*, 27 December, www.vox.com/2018/12/27/18137571/what-is-hopepunk-noblebright-grimdark (archived at https://perma.cc/Z2SJ-JKRT)

10 Chandler, S (2022) Proof of work is at the core of the system that manages bitcoin transactions and secures the network, *Business Insider*, 22 November, www.businessinsider.com/personal-finance/proof-of-work (archived at https://perma.cc/4Y6J-R8HG)

11 The Week (2022) 'Grim game of our times': What is sportswashing? 16 May, www.theweek.co.uk/news/sport/football/956759/what-is-sportswashing (archived at https://perma.cc/5Z73-UH7P)

12 Cheryl Chung, interview with the authors, 25 November 2022

13 Kleske, J (2022) Condensation of future imaginaries, *Futures Garden*, 26 June, garden.johanneskleske.com/condensation-of-future-imaginaries (archived at https://perma.cc/MG63-HQCP)

14 Schwartz, P (1991) *The Art of the Long View: Planning for the future in an uncertain world*, New York: Doubleday/Currency

15 Jeanette Kwek, interview with the authors, 18 November, 2022

16 Jeanette Kwek, interview with the authors, 18 November, 2022

17 Joanna Lepore, interview with the authors, 20 December 2022

18 Kent, S (1993) Words of Estimative Probability, Central Intelligence Agency, www.cia.gov/static/0aae8f84700a256abf63f7aad73b0a7d/Words-of-Estimative-Probability.pdf (archived at https://perma.cc/6K3W-K24V)

19 The Economist (2023) How to make sense of intelligence leaks, 9 March, www.economist.com/the-economist-explains/2023/03/09/how-to-make-sense-of-intelligence-leaks?utm_source=pocket_save (archived at https://perma.cc/5ZAH-G4SG)

20 Kent, S (1993) Words of Estimative Probability, Central Intelligence Agency, www.cia.gov/static/0aae8f84700a256abf63f7aad73b0a7d/Words-of-Estimative-Probability.pdf (archived at https://perma.cc/M577-KJFE)

21 IPCC (2005) Guidance notes for lead authors of the IPCC Fourth Assessment Report on Addressing Uncertainties, Intergovernmental Panel on Climate Change, July, www.ipcc.ch/site/assets/uploads/2018/02/ar4-uncertaintyguidancenote-1.pdf (archived at https://perma.cc/Y7TA-FFWM)

22 Joanna Lepore, interview with the authors, 20 December 2022

23 Joanna Lepore, interview with the authors, 20 December 2022

24 Mick Costigan, interview with the authors, 18 November 2022

25 BBC (nd) 1920s, History of the BBC, www.bbc.com/historyofthebbc/timelines/1920s/ (archived at https://perma.cc/8VBR-25M6)

26 BBC (nd) Learn more about what we do, About the BBC, www.bbc.co.uk/aboutthebbc/ (archived at https://perma.cc/U6NP-XMQJ)

27 BBC (nd) Our purpose, BBC Research & Development, www.bbc.co.uk/rd/about/our-purpose (archived at https://perma.cc/WJ46-Y6LZ)

28 Henry Cooke, interview with the authors, 22 December 2022

29 Libby Miller, interview with the authors, 22 December 2022

30 Henry Cooke, interview with the authors, 22 December 2022

31 Henry Cooke, interview with the authors, 22 December 2022

32 Henry Cooke, interview with the authors, 22 December 2022

33 Henry Cooke, interview with the authors, 22 December 2022

34 Libby Miller, interview with the authors, 22 December 2022

35 Libby Miller, interview with the authors, 22 December 2022

36 Miller, L and Cox, J (2022) Designing an object from the future for the BBC 100 collection, BBC Research & Development, 14 November, www.bbc.co.uk/rd/blog/2022-11-bbc-100-objects-collection-centenary (archived at https://perma.cc/5MFR-7NCT)

37 Miller, L and Cox, J (2022) Designing an object from the future for the BBC 100 collection, BBC Research & Development, 14 November, www.bbc.co.uk/rd/blog/2022-11-bbc-100-objects-collection-centenary (archived at https://perma.cc/QE9Z-8TYU)

38 Henry Cooke, interview with the authors, 22 December 2022

39 Miller, L and Cox, J (2022) Designing an object from the future for the BBC 100 collection, BBC Research & Development, 14 November, www.bbc.co.uk/rd/blog/2022-11-bbc-100-objects-collection-centenary (archived at https://perma.cc/FEL6-S8VD)

40 Miller, L and Cox, J (2022) Designing an object from the future for the BBC 100 collection, BBC Research & Development, 14 November, www.bbc.co.uk/rd/blog/2022-11-bbc-100-objects-collection-centenary (archived at https://perma.cc/C4PD-EC6K)

41 IWDA (nd) Imagining feminist futures after Covid-19, International Women's Development Agency, iwda.shorthandstories.com/imagining-feminist-futures-after-covid/index.html (archived at https://perma.cc/2HGZ-MRTW)

42 IWDA (nd) Imagining feminist futures after Covid-19, International Women's Development Agency, iwda.shorthandstories.com/imagining-feminist-futures-after-covid/index.html

43 Frost, R (2023) Exxon accurately predicted climate change in the 70s: Which other fossil fuel giants knew the risks? *Euronews*, 13 January, www.euronews.com/green/2023/01/13/exxon-accurately-predicted-climate-change-in-the-70s-which-other-fossil-fuel-giants-knew-t (archived at https://perma.cc/2NCP-RYH9)

Chapter 4: Tools and knowledge

1 Wack, P (1984) *Scenarios: The gentle art of re-perceiving : one thing or two learned while developing planning scenarios for Royal Dutch Shell*, Division of Research, Harvard Business School

2 Kennedy, J L and Putt, G H (1956) Administration of research in a research corporation, *Administrative Science Quarterly*, 1 (3), 326–39, doi.org/10.2307/2390927 (archived at https://perma.cc/J8B2-M5G3)

3 Sarpong, D, Maclean, M and Alexander, E (2013)'Organizing strategic foresight: A contextual practice of 'way finding', *Futures*, 53, 33–41, doi.org/10.1016/j.futures.2013.09.001 (archived at https://perma.cc/NCP8-9H7W)

4 Smith, S and Ashby, M (2020) *How to Future: Leading and sense-making in an age of hyperchange*, London; New York, NY: Kogan Page Inspire

5 Stein, S and Smith, S (2011) Ludic Foresight, YIRCoF '11: Yeditepe International Research Conference on Foresight, August

6 Stein, S and Smith, S (2011) Ludic Foresight, YIRCoF '11: Yeditepe International Research Conference on Foresight, August

7 How To Future (2020) How to future cards, www.howtofuture.com/cards (archived at https://perma.cc/F9DN-UGXX)

8 Artefact (nd) FUTREP – Original, Artefact Cards, artefactshop.com/products/futrep-original (archived at https://perma.cc/6BRL-DYWP)

9   London College of Communication (2022) Money from Mars, Workshop, www.eventbrite.co.uk/e/266184824977?aff=efbneb (archived at https://perma.cc/2YDC-N8HT)

10 Robinson, C (2020) Emerging Futures Fund announces £2 million in grants to diverse communities across the UK, The National Lottery Community Fund, 1 October, www.tnlcommunityfund.org.uk/news/blog/2020-10-01/emerging-futures-fund-announces-2-million-in-grants-to-diverse-communities-across-the-uk (archived at https://perma.cc/DF6C-5CSP)

11 Robinson, C (2020) Setting up a listening, learning & sense-making infrastructure at the National Lottery Community Fund, The National Lottery Community Fund, 3 June, www.tnlcommunityfund.org.uk/news/blog/2020-06-03/setting-up-a-listening-learning-sense-making-infrastructure-at-the-national-lottery-community-fund (archived at https://perma.cc/L3YW-ZM6Z)

12 Robinson, C (2021) A Cassie Quarterly, *Medium*, 18 April, cassierobinson.medium.com/a-cassie-quarterly-6adf038f7a2a (archived at https://perma.cc/7EJY-H35D)

13 Robinson, C (2023) *Futures Club* (email)

14 Robinson, C (2023) *Futures Club* (email)

15 Robinson, C (2022) Funding the third horizon, *Medium, 23 January*, medium.com/@cassierobinson/funding-the-third-horizon-ef76a60be9bb (archived at https://perma.cc/H752-TMB5)

16 Robinson, C (2020) Emerging Futures Fund announces £2 million in grants to diverse communities across the UK, The National Lottery Community Fund, 1 October, www.tnlcommunityfund.org.uk/news/blog/2020-10-01/emerging-futures-fund-announces-2-million-in-grants-to-diverse-communities-across-the-uk (archived at https://perma.cc/MSU8-ATD4)

17 Imagination Infrastructure is... (nd) www.imaginationinfrastructuring.com (archived at https://perma.cc/89CE-9KEP)

18 Imagination Infrastructure is... (nd) www.imaginationinfrastructuring.com (archived at https://perma.cc/38E8-8QXX)

19 Mick Costigan, interview with the authors, 18 January 2023

20 Discord (nd) About Discord: Our metrics, discord.com/company (archived at https://perma.cc/LJ7R-5UDG)

21 Julian Bleecker, interview with the authors, 24 January 2023

22 Julian Bleecker, interview with the authors, 24 January 2023

23 RADAR (nd) RADAR Wiki, https://radarxyz.notion.site/RADAR-Wiki-92959785c3174e5a91969d36a4336c29 (archived at https://perma.cc/Q55V-JSYK)

24 RADAR (2022) Join us in the future: (Re)introducing RADAR, 19 April, radar.mirror.xyz (archived at https://perma.cc/E83X-4KZW)

25 RADAR (2022) Join us in the future: (Re)introducing RADAR, 19 April, radar.mirror.xyz (archived at https://perma.cc/E83X-4KZW)

26 Henry Cooke, interview with the authors, 22 December 2022

27 Henry Cooke, interview with the authors, 22 December 2022

28 Matuschak, A (nd) Work with the garage door up, *Andy's Working Notes*, notes.andymatuschak.org/z21cgR9K3UcQ5a7yPsj2RUim3oM2TzdBByZu (archived at https://perma.cc/A4PW-69J2)

29 Johannes Kleske, Digital garden (email)

30 Henry Cooke, Digital garden (email)

31 Nesta (nd) Nesta's Trends Library, www.nesta.org.uk/project/discovery-hub/nestas-trends-library/ (archived at https://perma.cc/4D7C-5VU6)

32 Nesta – The UK's Innovation Agency (2022) Nesta's Trends Library Explained (online video), 3 October, www.youtube.com/watch?v=sewVDX_iNW4 (archived at https://perma.cc/VMC8-L69N)

33 UNDP (2021) United Nations Development Programme Strategic Plan 2022–2025, United Nations Development Programme, 2 September, www.undp.org/publications/undp-strategic-plan-2022-2025 (archived at https://perma.cc/GT9K-WB77)

34 UNDP (2021) United Nations Development Programme Strategic Plan 2022–2025: Phase 1: Landscape Paper, United Nations Development Programme, 15 January, www.undp.org/sites/g/files/zskgke326/files/migration/pe/311ada4f6b5d704c2ac91739430077b988621387c77686acb2d65dbb57ead8bb.pdf (archived at https://perma.cc/HLR7-CHE7)

35 UNDP (2022) Becoming anticipatory and future-fit across Asia and the Pacific, United Nations Development Programme, 12 January, www.undp.org/asia-pacific/news/becoming-anticipatory-and-future-fit-across-asia-and-pacific (archived at https://perma.cc/28WF-ZSYP)

36 UNDP (2021) Building a UNDP Futures Ecosystem, UNDP Executive Office, Strategy & Futures Team

37 UNDP (2021) Building a UNDP Futures Ecosystem, UNDP Executive Office, Strategy & Futures Team

38 UNDP (2021) Building a UNDP Futures Ecosystem, UNDP Executive Office, Strategy & Futures Team

39 Conway, M E (1968) How do committees invent? *Datamation*, 14 (4), 28–31

40 UNDP (2023) UNDP Signals Spotlight 2023: Insights from UNDP's Futures Network, United Nations Development Programme, New York, NY

41   UNDP (2023) UNDP Signals Spotlight 2023: Insights from UNDP's Futures
     Network, United Nations Development Programme, New York, NY

Chapter 5: Space and experience

1   Candy, S and Dunagan, J (2017) Designing an experiential scenario: *The people
    who vanished*, *Futures*, 86, 136–53, doi.org/10.1016/j.futures.2016.05.006
    (archived at https://perma.cc/Q24Y-NU39)
2   Candy, S and Dunagan, J (2017) Designing an experiential scenario: *The people
    who vanished*, *Futures*, 86, 136–53, doi.org/10.1016/j.futures.2016.05.006
    (archived at https://perma.cc/553A-3S96)
3   IFTF (2017) The American future gap survey, Institute for the Future, legacy.
    iftf.org/americanfuturegap/ (archived at https://perma.cc/3UL8-APAC)
4   Clark, A (2016) *Surfing Uncertainty: Prediction, action, and the embodied
    mind*, Oxford: Oxford University Press
5   McGonigal, J (2017) Our puny human brains are terrible at thinking about
    the future, *Slate*, 13 April, slate.com/technology/2017/04/why-people-are-so-
    bad-at-thinking-about-the-future.html (archived at https://perma.cc/8AKM-
    TTYH)
6   McGonigal, J (2017) Our puny human brains are terrible at thinking about
    the future, *Slate*, 13 April, slate.com/technology/2017/04/why-people-are-so-
    bad-at-thinking-about-the-future.html (archived at https://perma.cc/8AKM-
    TTYH)
7   Atance, C M and O'Neill, D K (2001) Episodic future thinking, *Trends in
    Cognitive Sciences*, 5 (12), 533–9, doi.org/10.1016/S1364-6613(00)01804-0
    (archived at https://perma.cc/DGH5-C5CJ)
8   McGonigal, J (2022) *Imaginable: How to see the future coming and feel ready
    for anything – even things that seem impossible today*, New York: Spiegel and
    Grau
9   Slaughter, R A and Bussey, M (2006) *Futures thinking for social foresight*,
    Indooroopilly, Qld: Tamkang University Press/Foresight International
10 Dubai Future Foundation (2022) Dubai Future Forum (online video), 11
    October, www.youtube.com/watch?v=ZnU5v7v69j4 (archived at https://
    perma.cc/7RE7-Y2LS)
11 Dubai Future Foundation (2022) Dubai Future Forum (online video), 11
    October, www.youtube.com/watch?v=ZnU5v7v69j4 (archived at https://
    perma.cc/SCH7-5HYE)

12   Dorkenwald, S (2023) Superflux: Space of possibilities, *nomad*, 13, www.
the-nomad-magazine.com/superflux-space-of-possibilities/ (archived at https://
perma.cc/3R6C-ZTJZ)

13   Jon Ardern and Anab Jain, interview with the authors, 31 January 2023

14   Bosch, T (2012) Sci-fi writer Bruce Sterling explains the intriguing new
concept of design fiction, *Slate*, 2 March, slate.com/technology/2012/03/
bruce-sterling-on-design-fictions.html (archived at https://perma.cc/P6A7-
BTL9)

15   Foster, N (2013) The future mundane, Core77, 7 October, core77.com/
posts/25678/The-Future-Mundane (archived at https://perma.cc/8WC2-F7Z2)

16   Sterling, B (2009) Design fiction, *Interactions*, 16 (3), 20–4, doi.org/10.1145/
1516016.1516021 (archived at https://perma.cc/V6PP-ZW6U)

17   Jon Ardern, interview with the authors, 31 January 2023

18   Julian Bleecker (2022) *Near Future Laboratory podcast* – episode 41, Design
fiction with Elliott P Montgomery, podcasts.apple.com/us/podcast/n-41-
design-fiction-with-elliott-p-montgomery/id1546452193?i=1000568754365
(archived at https://perma.cc/5JTQ-ML2K)

19   Dorkenwald, S (2023) Superflux: Space of possibilities, *nomad*, 13, www.the-
nomad-magazine.com/superflux-space-of-possibilities/ (archived at https://
perma.cc/AL8S-B4FX)

20   Nesta (2019) Futures artefacts, www.nesta.org.uk/project/community-
resilience-in-emergencies/futures-artefacts/ (archived at https://perma.cc/
SS26-ZJ5D)

21   Smith, S (2018) Speculative humanitarian futures: Imagining responses to a
turbulent world, *Phase Change*, 14 September, medium.com/phase-change/
speculative-humanitarian-futures-9ce9a76dbf38 (archived at https://perma.
cc/9AW9-AGUK)

22   Girardin, F (2022) An archeology for the future in space, *Design Fictions*,
14 July, medium.com/design-fictions/an-archeology-for-the-future-in-
space-9e5273923184 (archived at https://perma.cc/M3EK-YN2S)

23   Bleecker, J et al (2022) *The Manual of Design Fiction*, Venice, CA: Near Future
Laboratory

24   Tellart (2014) Future government services, www.tellart.com/projects/
mofgs-2014 (archived at https://perma.cc/2X9H-AQHK)

25   Smith, S (2017) Designing Dubai's futures, *Phase Change*, 13 March, https://
medium.com/phase-change/designing-dubais-futures-d3bebb0998ad (archived
at https://perma.cc/8SJP-P8BQ)

26 Dr Noah Raford, interview with the authors, 15 November 2022
27 Dr Noah Raford, interview with the authors, 15 November 2022

Chapter 6: Rules and norms

1 Gulf News (2022) 'The future belongs to those who can imagine it' – Sheikh
   Mohammed's quotes on Dubai's Museum of the Future inspires beholders,
   15 February, gulfnews.com/uae/the-future-belongs-to-those-who-can-imagine-
   it---sheikh-mohammeds-quotes-on-dubais-museum-of-the-future-inspires-
   beholders-1.85736312 (archived at https://perma.cc/3NRU-6YCZ)

2 GlobalData (nd) International Business Machines Corp company profile,
   www.globaldata.com/company-profile/international-business-machines-corp/
   (archived at https://perma.cc/G4LN-BY8Z)

3 McElroy, N G (2021) The innovative engine of IBM's design philosophy,
   Fortune, 7 September, fortune.com/2021/09/07/new-ibm-design-director-
   katrina-alcorn-phil-gilbert/ (archived at https://perma.cc/DEN2-42R7)

4 Meghan McGrath, interview with the authors, 9 December 2022

5 IBM100 (2012) The making of International Business Machines, www-03.
   ibm.com/ibm/history/ibm100/us/en/icons/makingibm/impacts/ (archived at
   https://perma.cc/QNF6-9HXX)

6 They Create Worlds (2014) Historical interlude: The birth of the computer, part
   3, the commercialization of the computer, 26 February, videogamehistorian.
   wordpress.com/tag/tom-watson-sr/ (archived at https://perma.cc/R8QJ-G5NN)

7 They Create Worlds (2014) Historical interlude: The birth of the computer, part 3,
   the commercialization of the computer, 26 February, videogamehistorian.
   wordpress.com/tag/tom-watson-sr/ (archived at https://perma.cc/R8QJ-G5NN)

8 Meghan McGrath, interview with the authors, 9 December 2022

9 Dan Silveira, interview with the authors, 29 November 2022

10 Dan Silveira and Roosevelt Faulkner, interview with the authors, 29 November
   2022

11 Dan Silveira and Roosevelt Faulkner, interview with the authors, 29 November
   2022

12 Meghan McGrath, interview with the authors, 9 December 2022

13 Grim, T (2009) Foresight maturity model (FMM): Achieving best practices in
   the foresight field, *Journal of Futures Studies*, 13 (4), 69–80, wfsf.org/foresight-
   maturity-model-terry-grim-2009/ (archived at https://perma.cc/4FE8-8YHL)

14   Smith, S (2021) Mapping impacts and implications, *Practical Futuring*, 8
      December, medium.com/practical-futuring/mapping-impacts-and-implications-
      74e737312191 (archived at https://perma.cc/8SK2-C9RQ)
15   Inayatullah, S (2004) *The causal layered analysis (CLA) reader: Theory and
      case studies of an integrative and transformative methodology*, Taipei:
      Tamkang University Press
16   Meghan McGrath, interview with the authors, 9 December 2022
17   Meghan McGrath, interview with the authors, 9 December 2022

Chapter 7: Networks and ecosystems

1   Moore, J F (1993) Predators and prey: A new ecology of competition, *Harvard
     Business Review*, 1 May, hbr.org/1993/05/predators-and-prey-a-new-ecology-
     of-competition (archived at https://perma.cc/UBZ5-TVB6)
2   Joanna Lepore, interview with the authors, 20 December 2022
3   RAND Corporation (nd) A brief history of RAND, www.rand.org/about/
     history.html (archived at https://perma.cc/Q5PV-6P66)
4   IFTF (nd) About IFTF, Institute for the Future, www.iftf.org/about-iftf/
     (archived at https://perma.cc/ELE5-XKJD)
5   Brandenburger, A and Nalebuff, B (2021) The rules of co-opetition, *Harvard
     Business Review*, 1 January, hbr.org/2021/01/the-rules-of-co-opetition
     (archived at https://perma.cc/5ZNZ-JVZT)
6   AXA (nd) Profile and key figures, www.axa.com/en/about-us/key-figures
     (archived at https://perma.cc/US5A-WAR5)
7   Olivier Desbiey, interview with the authors, 19 December 2022
8   Olivier Desbiey, interview with the authors, 19 December 2022
9   Olivier Desbiey, interview with the authors, 19 December 2022
10   Olivier Desbiey, interview with the authors, 19 December 2022
11   AXA (2022) *Welcome to ProgressLand*, 17 February, www.axa.com/en/
      news/2022-AXA-Foresight-Report (archived at https://perma.cc/C6SW-JJRW)
12   Olivier Desbiey, interview with the authors, 19 December 2022
13   Copenhagen Institute for Futures Studies (2022), LinkedIn, www.linkedin.
      com/posts/cphfutures_futuresthinking-partnership-insurance-activity-
      6983017507489992704-Lh-3 (archived at https://perma.cc/FT6E-XJRQ)
14   Olivier Desbiey, interview with the authors, 19 December 2022

Conclusion

1 Ogilvy, J (2011) Facing the fold: From the eclipse of Utopia to the restoration of hope, *Foresight*, 13 (4), 7–23, doi.org/10.1108/14636681111153931 (archived at https://perma.cc/XA8E-VDPJ)

2 Krishnan, A (2022) The masters tools will never dismantle the masters house, *Medium*, 22 November, aarathi-krishnan.medium.com/the-masters-tools-will-never-dismantle-the-masters-house-fa9900ef312f (archived at https://perma.cc/J5KE-YNZ3)

Index